7 PERFECT Ste

How YOU Can Achieve Your Dreams

By

Bob Dudley and Cathy Dudley

For I know the plans that I have for you," says the LORD, "plans to prosper you and not of evil towards you, plans to give you a hopeful future." Jeremiah 29:11

All biblical translations are taken from the King James Version of the Bible or are the direct translations of the authors from the Hebrew or Greek texts.

Life Changers 180, LLC
Attn: *7 PERFECT Steps to Success*
55 Christians Dr.
Hanover, PA 17331

ISBN: 154242478X
ISBN-13: 978-1542424783

DEDICATION

This book is dedicated to our daughters Robin, Tina, Susan and Melissa, our granddaughters, Madison and Bliss, and our grandsons, Julian and Joseph. All ladies and gentlemen who we are very proud of.

CONTENTS

Preface – Why Should You Listen to Me

The books on personal motivation and success seem to fall into two different categories:

> There are those books written by people looking on from the outside. These books try to explain, from observing successful people, how to become successful yourself. Some of the better authors (though successful in their own right) who take this approach are Napoleon Hill, Anthony Robbins, Thomas Stanley, Mark Victor Hanson and T Harv Eker.

> The second group is a collection of books by people who have written about their own successes. These are a look from the inside. Authors in this group include Donald Trump, David Lindahl and Robert Kiyosaki.

I fall into the second group. And, as way of introduction, I would like to briefly tell you my story. My childhood was less than impressive. My father left us when I was about a year old. I never met him. By the time I was

18-years-old, I had attended 17 different schools throughout California, Texas and Massachusetts as we moved from one housing project to another. I had two step-fathers. I had two half-sisters, three half-brothers and one step-brother. I turned 18 in January of 1975. That same month I quit high school – I was fed up with life. And, to celebrate turning 18, my parents took me to the local welfare office to sign up for benefits. That was when I left home and, eventually, joined the US Army.

I spent three years in the army. In that time, I received my GED and a high school diploma. I also earned a black belt in Tae Kwon Do while stationed in Korea. After finishing my time in the army I moved to Pontiac, MI to face a major shift in my life.

I moved to Pontiac to attend Midwestern Baptist College. I knew I wanted to go to college but I didn't know what I wanted to major in. My pastor in the army suggested I go to a bible college until I made up my mind. He had gone to Midwestern so I went there. During my sophomore year I had what can only be described as a life changing crisis. I had this deep feeling of failure in my life. I had quit high school. I felt I had quit the army (they put a LOT of pressure on you to re-enlist but I refused) and now I was thinking about quitting bible college. I decided I needed a challenge to prove to myself that I wasn't a quitter.

I also felt I needed to know there was something inside me that could accomplish a task. I knew my mother's side of the family did not give me what it took – after all, I spent most of my youth travelling from housing project to housing project as my parents avoided paying any bills. I decided to track down my natural father to see if he could be a source of inspiration. What a disaster. I finally tracked him down in Seattle, WA. We talked on the phone for about 5 minutes. A worse-than-useless conversation. He didn't even remember which sister he had married – my mom or my Aunt Edna. There would be no motivational help from that side of my family tree.

If I was going to do something useful with my life it had to come from me, personally. I decided to enroll in Oakland University and to finish whatever degree I applied for. At registration they asked me what I wanted to major in. I picked up a catalog and thumbed through it. Physics sounded hard, I had no idea what it was, but it sounded hard – and, for whatever reason, I needed to do the hardest thing I could find to once-and-for-all prove to myself that I wasn't worthless. I told the lady I wanted to get a degree in Physics.

You know, to take your first Physics class, you need to be enrolled in Calculus. At the time, I didn't even know that Calculus was a math class. After the math placement exam I had to start so far down in the math courses it would, theoretically, take two years just to get enough math to start in my chosen major. And, on top of all that, I was working full time at a factory on second shift. But, I was determined I could do it.

Long story short, I ended up graduating at the top of my class with a degree in Physics after just three years. After this, I felt I could do *ANYTHING* I set my mind to. Although I didn't know it at the time, this was the start of my discovery of the ***7 PERFECT Steps to Success***.

Over the next 30 years I was unstoppable. I

accomplished everything I set my mind to. If I decided I wanted to do something, I would just jump in with both feet and dominate. Here is a partial list of some of my achievements:

Formal Education:

BS Physics (departmental honors)
BS Aerospace Engineering (Magna Cum Laude)
MS Astronautical Engineering
MA Biblical Studies (Magna Cum Laude)
ThD Biblical Studies

Physical Accomplishments:

4th Degree Black Belt – WTF Tae Kwon Do
2nd Degree Black Belt –Tang Soo Do
1st Degree Black Belt – ITF Tae Kwon Do
1st Degree Black Belt – Kuntaw
1st Degree Black Belt – Jujitsu
Professional Ballroom Dance Instructor (15 years)

Career:

Air Force: After getting my degree in Physics, I joined the US Air Force as a rocket scientist (astronautical engineer). I retired at the rank of Major with 20 years of service.

I formed and managed a chain of five martial arts studios (Side Kicks Taekwondo).

I worked as a ballroom dance instructor for 15 years for a major dance chain in the United States.

While serving as a master instructor of

aerospace engineering at the United States Naval Academy, I sailed a 44 foot sloop to Bermuda and back with another officer and a group of eight midshipmen.

After retiring from the Air Force, I worked with an aerospace software company until I formed my own aerospace software consulting firm: Dudley Consulting.

I founded two evangelism organizations (Agora Evangelism Ministries, Inc and the Lura B Walker Foundation, Inc). The Lura B Walker Foundation still does evangelism training around the world. We train pastors to refocus their churches to have an evangelistic outlook.

My wife, Cathy, and I formed a real estate investment company called the John H Woodburn Group, Inc (named after her father). We own property (as of this writing) in three different states – Pennsylvania, Maryland and Ohio.

Books Written:

Tae Kwon Do Text Book (1981) – Training manual for the owners of the Side Kicks Martial Arts studios.

Introduction to Satellite Design (1995) – Classified training manual for the National Cryptologic School at Ft Meade, MD.

Christian Growth (2010) – A discipleship book for new Christians.

Gold Represents Heaven (2013) – A step-by-step guide to using colors in your gospel presentation.

The Gospel, Evangelism, and God's Heart: Why This is Important to EVERY Christian (2014) – This book was a #1 Bestseller.

Everyday Evangelism (2014) – A non-threatening and very effective method for sharing your faith.

7 PERFECT Steps to Success: How YOU Can Achieve Your Dreams (2017) – The very book you are holding.

Awards and Memberships:

Lifetime member of Mensa
Defense Meritorious Service Medal
Navy Meritorious Service Medal
Air Force Meritorious Service Medal

As you can see, I have had a fairly busy life. Over the last 30 years I have been able to accomplish anything "I put my mind to." At first, my formula for success seemed mostly instinctive. In the last few years, however, I have begun to see a pattern that was consistent in all of my accomplishments and the accomplishments of others that I have studied. I saw that pattern in the people I have interviewed. And, I saw that pattern repeated in several places in the Bible.

In the next few pages, I would like to share that pattern with you. I hope it is as rewarding and invigorating to you as it has been to me.

Introduction

And it came to pass on a certain day, as he was teaching, that there were Pharisees and doctors of the law sitting by, which were come out of every town of Galilee, and Judaea, and Jerusalem: and the power of the Lord was present to heal them. And, behold, men brought in a bed a man which was taken with a palsy: and they sought means to bring him in, and to lay him before him. And when they could not find by what way they might bring him in because of the multitude, they went upon the housetop, and let him down through the tiling with his couch into the midst before Jesus. **And when he saw their faith**, *he said unto him, Man, thy sins are forgiven thee. (Luke 5:7-20)*

I've often wondered what possessed these men to go to such extreme lengths to help their friend and bring him to Jesus. What was their motivation? Where did their faith come from? What drove them to get on the roof and lower their friend to Jesus when most people would have said, "Oh, well. We tried. But the crowd is too big. Maybe we can come back another day."

Over the last couple of years my wife, Cathy, and I have shifted our focus in life. In the words of Robert Kiyosaki, we went from the E-quadrant to the B-quadrant; we went from being employees to business owners. This not only took a tremendous shift in our thought processes, it also took a tremendous amount of drive and faith. As we became more and more successful and closer to financial freedom (when our passive income equaled our expenses), I began to ask myself if there was a pattern that others could follow. I read, extensively, the Bible, the self-help books and the motivational books that are out there. I studied books on how self-made millionaires got to be where they are.

As I studied, I began to see similarities between myself, other self-made millionaires and the friends in the gospel account above. I eventually broke down the path to success into seven steps. These steps are really a set of spiritual laws. And, just like physical laws (gravity, electro-magnetism and others), these spiritual laws apply to everyone. If you follow these steps you WILL be successful. And, just as God can intervene to suspend the physical laws, the only way you can fail is if God suspends these spiritual laws. I have broken the ***7 PERFECT Steps to Success*** into an acrostic:

Precious Burning Desire
Exercise Your Faith Not Your Fear
Repeat After Me
Firsthand Knowledge
Effective Planning
Concrete Action
Tenacious Persistence

The first two steps in success are internal. You must have a dream, a *Precious Burning Desire*, to accomplish your goal in life. You also need to have complete faith you can accomplish it. At the same time, you need to overcome your fears. All of this happens inside of us. And, before we move out into the world, we have to make sure the will and attitude of our hearts and minds are prepared.

The next three steps help us to move from the inside to the outside. I call the first of these steps, Repeat After Me. Basically, we will talk about how to reinforce our faith and begin to "make our dreams a reality". We will look at how to start to turn our dreams and our faith into something real and tangible. We'll then talk about the next step, gaining the knowledge you need to move forward. And, for the last step in this section, we will talk about turning your knowledge into a workable plan of attack.

Once you have the right mental attitude and have gained the knowledge needed and built your plan, it is time to act. This is the last two steps. I have met way too many people that have accomplished the first five steps only to fail in the last two. You MUST take concrete action and you MUST have tenacious persistence. In other words, you have to act and keep acting!

I invite you to read the pages of this book, experiment with the seven steps, and see what great things you can do in your life.

Going for the Gold

Going for the Gold! In this section, we are going to learn how to win the inner game of success. We call this section "Going for the Gold" because the two steps in this section are THE most important steps to achieving success in your life. Before you are ready to transform the world around you, you must undergo a transformation within you. In this section, we are going to talk about two things – how to have a *Precious Burning Desire* to accomplish whatever task is before you and how to have the unwavering faith to believe that you WILL succeed.

I. Precious Burning Desire

Where there is no vision, the people perish: (Proverbs 29:18)

Have you ever wanted something so bad you could taste it? Have you ever wanted something so bad that you could think of nothing else? Your desire was so all consuming, it was useless to try to concentrate on anything else? If you have ever felt this way then you have felt a *Precious Burning Desire.* This desire is the first step to becoming unstoppable.

Bob's Story

It was April 1, 1983. I was standing on the parade grounds with hundreds of other officer trainees at Lackland AFB, San Antonio, TX. I was about to be commissioned as a 2nd Lieutenant in the United States Air Force. While we stood there waiting to throw our hats in the air, I had time to reflect on the very rough road that brought me to this honorable day.

Lura Walker, a high school dropout, was 20 years old when she became pregnant from her 29 year old boyfriend.

Right away, they went to the Justice of the Peace, got a marriage license, and were married. Nine months later I was born to Robert Lloyd and Lura Belle Dudley on January 5, 1957 in Torrance, CA outside of Los Angeles. I would never really know my father. By the time I was 2 years old, my mom and dad had gone their separate ways. The first man I knew as my father was Eddie O'Connell - my first step-father. I can recall, like it was yesterday, how I found out he was not my natural father. Eddie was in the Navy and we were living in Corpus Christi, TX. I was in first grade and my parents were having a very heated argument. I became scared and ran to my "father". My mom said (I can hear her voice 50 years later), "I don't know why you are going to him. He's not your father." Yes, to hurt him she hurt me. My whole world just collapsed.

As devastating as this revelation was, it really hit home the next year. My mom and "dad" were getting a divorce. My mom moved (with me, my half-sister and my half-brother) to San Diego. It was Christmas and my mom set up for us kids to go to our grandparents (Eddie's parents) for Christmas. On Christmas morning the three of us woke up excited to see what Santa had brought for us. I sat and watched my brother and sister open present after present. There was nothing for me. Even at 7 years old, I knew that I didn't belong to Eddie's family. I cried for weeks.

The next year we moved to Oceanside, CA. My mom worked as a telephone operator. After school, my sister, brother and I would go to the babysitter until my mom came home. One Wednesday my mom didn't show up to get us. Thursday came and went with no mom. On Friday I overheard the babysitter telling someone on the phone that we would be picked up by child services, if no one showed up for us by Monday. That weekend we were picked up by my Aunt Pat (my mom's sister). We lived with her and her six daughters for about a year.

Over the next few years we moved from relative to relative with intermittent periods with my mom. This continued until my mom married Andy Anderson. I was 12 years old at the time. We still moved a lot. Every time our rent would be way overdue, we would move to a new place. By the time I was 18 years old and a senior in high school, I had gone to 17 different schools.

By the middle of my senior year, I was already signing up for classes at my third school of the year. The counselor informed me I would have to repeat my senior year since I missed so much school. It was at that moment I decided to quit. Since I was 18 years old and out of school, my parents decided to take me down to the local welfare office for me to sign up for benefits. At this point I knew I had to get out of this environment. I left home and joined the Army. It was the summer of 1975.

I earned my GED and finished high school while stationed in South Korea. Then, after three years in the infantry, I moved to Pontiac, MI to go to Midwestern Baptist College. I stayed there for three semesters before I realized Bible college wasn't for me at that time of my life.

Here is where my life changed forever. I tapped into something that I didn't even understand until years later. I felt like a loser, a quitter. I looked at my life and wondered why I ever thought I would amount to anything. I needed to know there was something inside me that would warrant trying to make something of myself. I tracked down the father I never knew. I found out he lived in Seattle, WA. I was able to get his phone number and I called him. I needed (so I thought) to feel like there was something from his side of my family that would give me the drive to continue. Boy, I really set myself up for disappointment. My father could not even remember which sister he married back in the 1950's - my mom or my Aunt Edna.

As I hung up the phone, tears streaming down my cheeks, something snapped inside me. I was at a crossroads in my life. I could either accept the inevitable and find a job in a local factory/store (even go back on welfare) where I would waste away and be one of the faceless masses. Or, I could rise above this massive depression and prove to myself once and for all I could be a success. I opted to prove that I could be successful. I wanted it so bad I could taste it. I wanted it so bad I could think of nothing else. My desire to prove I could accomplish something was so all consuming, it was useless to try to concentrate on anything else.

That week I signed up for classes at the local university - Oakland University. At registration they asked me what I wanted to major in. I picked up a catalog off the desk and thumbed through the pages. I wanted something hard, I wanted something that was challenging, I wanted something that would prove I could accomplish ANYTHING. Physics - I saw the word jump out of the page. I had no idea what Physics was. But, boy, it sure sounded hard. I told the nice lady that I wanted to major in Physics.

Well, when you get a degree in Physics you have to be good at math - who knew? They had me take a math placement test. I had to take algebra I, algebra II, analytical functions, and trigonometry before I could even take the calculus class that was a foundation for my first Physics class. All of this while I had to provide for a family and worked full time at a factory outside of Detroit.

But, I had determined this was going to happen. I WAS going to get a BS in Physics. I had a singleness of purpose and a drive that seemed, at times, supernatural.

Not only did I get that degree, I did it in three years and graduated with honors. The day of graduation I was on an airplane to Lackland AFB to become an officer in the United States Air Force - I KNEW, beyond a shadow of a doubt, I could do anything I put my mind to.

And now, I know I can show you how to have that same confidence and that same success.

Nehemiah

Nehemiah is one of my favorite Bible heroes. Nehemiah started out as the cup bearer of King Artaxerxes of Persia. He lived during the time of the Jewish captivity. The nation of Judah had been defeated by the Persians and he was now living in the Persian palace in Shushan.

One day some men from Judah were in the palace. Nehemiah, curious about his homeland, asked them for news of Jerusalem. And, the news was grim. The walls of Jerusalem had crumbled to the ground and all the gates had been consumed in fire. In other words, Jerusalem was completely vulnerable to attack. He knew a city with no walls was a city on borrowed time. This was his city. This was the City of David. This city represented the promises of God.

The sorry condition of Jerusalem was so devastating to Nehemiah that he wept for days. He cried out to God and mourned. He asked God to forgive his sins. He asked God to forgive the sins of the entire nation of Israel. He reminded God of God's promise to restore Israel if they would only repent. He then did a strange thing. Instead of begging God to restore Jerusalem, he asked God to give him, Nehemiah, favor with the king.

Why did he do this? Why did Nehemiah ask God to give him favor in front of the king? He had a *Precious Burning Desire.*

As the king's cup bearer, he was called before the king. In the past, Nehemiah was always happy. As a matter of fact, the king would not allow anyone who was not in a good mood to be in front of him. To appear before the king in a negative mood was punishable by death. But, God answered Nehemiah's prayer and he had favor before King Artaxerxes. The king asked Nehemiah why his countenance was down. Nehemiah silently prayed to God then told the king about the waste and destruction of Jerusalem. He asked the king if he, Nehemiah, could return to Jerusalem to build it up.

Nehemiah's desire to see Jerusalem restored was so all consuming that he did not want to leave it to anyone else to accomplish. And, he was allowed to return to Jerusalem.

In the following months, as Nehemiah rebuilt the walls of Jerusalem, he faced many obstacles. He faced ridicule, force, discouragement, fear, guile, slander, and threats. But, none of this stopped him.

Nehemiah wanted to see the walls of Jerusalem

restored so bad he could taste it. He wanted the walls of Jerusalem restored so bad he could think of nothing else. His desire was so all consuming, it was useless to try to concentrate on anything else. He felt a *Precious Burning Desire.* His desire was the first step to becoming unstoppable.

WHAT IS A PRECIOUS BURNING DESIRE?

A burning desire is NOT just a burning wish. It's not enough to wish that something will happen. It's not enough to say, "I wish I could be a missionary." It's not enough to say, "I wish I could have a loving spouse." It's not enough to say, "I wish I could make a million dollars." There's a massive difference between *wish* and *will.* You have to move beyond just a wish and have a *Precious Burning Desire.*

The best way to describe this *Precious Burning Desire* is to relate a story given by Pastor Eric Thomas in a motivational speech to a group of students.

> There was a young man who wanted to make a lot of money so he went to a guru. He told the guru, "I wanna be on the same level you are."
>
> The guru said, "If you want to be on the same level I'm on, I'll meet you tomorrow at 4 A.M. at the beach."
>
> So the young man arrived there at 4 A.M. He was ready to rock n' roll. He had on a suit but should have worn shorts.
>
> The old man grabs his hand and says: "How bad do you want to be successful?"

He said: "Real bad."

The guru said, "Walk on out in the water." So he walks out into the water.

When he walks out to the water they make it to waist deep and he thinks, "This guy is crazy. I wanna make money and he has me out here swimming. I didn't ask to be a lifeguard. I wanna make money."

The guru says, "Come on a little further," They walked out a little further - the water was right around the shoulder area. The young man thought, "This old man is crazy - he might be making money but he's crazy."

The guru says, "Come on out a little further." Since the guru still held his hand, the young man went out a little further. The water was now right at his mouth.

The young man started to pull back and the old man said: "I thought you said you wanted to be successful."

He said: "I do."

The guru said, "Then walk a little further."

Then the guru grabbed the young man's head and held him under water. He held him down, and held him down. The young man began to panic and started trying to claw and scratch the guru. But the guru kept holding his head under water. Just before the young man was about to pass out, he raised him up out of the water.

The guru said: "When you want to succeed as bad as you want to breathe then you will be successful."

"When you want to succeed as much as you want to breath." When I heard this illustration, I knew I had a handle on what a *Precious Burning Desire* is. Imagine how hard you would struggle to breath if you could not catch your breath. I saw a poster once that said, "Obsession is a word the lazy use to describe the dedicated."

The Apostle Paul told the church in Corinth, "For though I preach the gospel, I have nothing to glory of: for necessity is laid upon me; yea, woe is unto me, if I preach not the gospel!" He was saying that he was obsessed with giving the gospel. He was dedicated and couldn't think of doing anything else. He was saying he couldn't conceive of doing anything else but giving the gospel. He wanted to give the gospel as much as he wanted to breath. He had a *Precious Burning Desire* to give the gospel. He didn't just *wish* he could give the gospel, he *had* to give the gospel.

If you want to be successful, you need to have this same obsession as the young man that wanted to breath. You have to have the same obsession as Paul. Whatever burning desire you have in mind, it must be all consuming.

Why Dream Big

When your dreams are bigger than life, over the top, they are like a large beach ball rolling over little toy wooden blocks. You can obliterate any obstacle in your way. When your dreams are small, like a marble trying to knock down those same blocks, obstacles are overwhelming and impossible to overcome.

Think about it…When you have a dream that is SOOOO big it will easily consume your obstacles, it becomes easier to make decisions, easier to say *no* to the things that don't accomplish your big dream, overcome things that push you out of your comfort zone. You are able to move more obstacles more frequently and at a faster rate.

Why can't we have a dream that consumes the obstacles of life? The only way to do this is to have an over the top, larger than life dream. The beach ball, the BIG DREAM, knocks down multiple blocks, obstacles, in one easy throw.

With a *Precious Burning Desire*, you will have the courage to ask people to help you knock down obstacles. With a *Precious Burning Desire*, you will be drawn to like-minded people who will strategize with you to make your dream a reality. A *Precious Burning Desire* helps propel you to success. It helps to stomp out any obstacle in the way to accomplishing your heart's desire.

"Why Not?"

Robin Strempek, CEO of Life Changers 180, has an interesting take on dreaming big. The way she says it is, "Why not dream big?" She says, "Imagine the impact you could have on your life if you asked yourself, 'Why not?'. Better yet, imagine the impact you could have on others ideas and dreams if you asked them why not?"

She put this philosophy to practice with her daughter, Madison. Let me share what happened…

Madison came to her mom one day and asked her

mom to buy her some lipstick (Madison was about 8-years-old at the time). Her mom told her there was enough lipstick around the house, she didn't need to get anything new. About an hour later Madison came back and asked her mom, "Would it be OK if I made my own lipstick? I found out how to make it from YouTube."

Robin said, "Why not?" They went to the store to get the supplies. They spent more than the cost of lipstick. But, Robin was teaching Madison more than beauty tips. She was growing an entrepreneur.

The lipstick experiment was a total success. Madison made several different colors. She sold some. She even had a salon agree to sell some of her products on consignment.

The real frosting on the cake came when Madison wrote her first book at the age of 10. And, at the age of 11, Madison's book became a #1 bestseller. If you are interested in seeing how the "why not?" philosophy turned a tragic event in Madison's life into something extraordinary, her book is called, "Everyone Makes Mistakes: Living with My Daddy in Jail."

But, what do you do if you share your *Precious Burning Desire* and someone says, "Why? Why would you do that?" and they begin to ridicule your idea. My advice is easy to tell you about, it's not so easy to pull off (at least, inside your heart). Basically, just tell them, "Thank you for sharing." Then walk away realizing people laughed at the guy who invented the pool noodle and now he's a millionaire.

How to Dream Big

Hopefully, by now, you are starting to see why you need a *Precious Burning Desire.* You might even have a few insights of our own concerning YOUR *Precious Burning Desire*, your big dream. It's one thing to know WHY we should dream big and to relate stories of people who have become famous through their big dreams. It's another thing to know HOW to dream big, how to have your own *Precious Burning Desire.*

All of us know how to think. We do it every day. But, going from just thinking to thinking BIG, to developing your own *Precious Burning Desire*, is like going from a walk around the block to running a full marathon. It's doable but a lot of us just don't know how to do it on our own. For the next few pages, I want to show you how to set yourself up for a *Precious Burning Desire* you will be able to turn into a reachable goal.

Conscious and Subconscious: Friend or Foe?

Before we dig into the actual mechanics of how to dream big, we need to talk a bit about who we are and how we are made up. In particular, I want to spend a moment talking about the conscious, the subconscious, and a couple of laws that relate the two. The conscious only takes up about 10% of our mind. The subconscious takes up the other 90% - something we really need to know about.

The Conscious Mind: Your conscious mind acts as the CPU of your body, like the brains of a computer. I like what Brian Tracy says about the conscious mind – it identifies, compares, and analyzes data from the outside world. The conscious mind determines your world view and what gets through to our subconscious.

The Subconscious Mind: Your subconscious is like the hard drive. It stores EVERYTHING you ever took in through your senses. It just stores and retrieves data. Your subconscious does not have a mind of its own. It does whatever the conscious mind tells it to do. One of the functions of the subconscious (that we need to worry about now) is, it defines our comfort zone. When we are asked to do something that makes us feel uneasy it is because our subconscious is telling us the action is not part of our normal operations.

There are three laws relating to these two parts of our mind which we need to understand before we can build our big dreams.

The Law of Subconscious Activity: Any idea or thought you accept as true in your conscious mind will be accepted without question by your subconscious mind. And, your subconscious mind will immediately begin working to bring it into your reality. Henry Ford said, "If you think you can, you're right. And, if you think you can't, you're also right." This law is what he was talking about. Your subconscious mind will move heaven and earth to make your perception of you come true.

The Law of Concentration: Whatever you dwell on grows and expands in your life. Some professors did an experiment where they put people in a room where they never were in before. They asked the people to memorize everything red in the room. Then, when they took them out of the room, they were asked to describe everything they saw that was yellow. They could hardly remember anything yellow.

The Law of Substitution: Your conscious mind can only hold one thought at a time and you can substitute one thought for another. Here is a great experiment in multi-tasking. Draw two long lines on a piece of paper, left to right. On the top line you are going to write the numbers 1 to 26. On the lower line you are going to write the alphabet from A to Z. Here's the catch, write "1" then "A", write "2" then "B". Keep this up through the entire alphabet, timing yourself. Do the exercise again. But this time, write out all of the numbers. Then write out all of the letters. Again, time yourself. You will be surprised how fast you are the second time compared to the first.

Most of us have spent our lives, so far, as victims of these laws. What we are going to do today is take advantage of these laws and turn the tables on them.

Comfort or Cringe?

This may seem overly obvious when I say it but, most of us are motivated to move towards comfort and to avoid, what I like to call, cringe. But here's the thing, what some people consider a comfort, others might consider a cringe.

For example, my wife, Cathy, loves to plan out every meal for the week. She is a person who loves a very stable life – she hates variability. I, on the other hand, never want to decide what to eat until just before the meal – I like variety and variability, I can't stand stability. I don't like making plans for the day, because then the word "premeditated" gets thrown around in court. My comfort is her cringe. My cringe is her comfort.

When we started our success coaching company, ***Life Changers 180***, we wanted to help people be successful like we were (there was Robin Strempek and myself, and all of the mentors as they came on board). The easy part, for us, was standing in front of a large audience telling them the "secrets" to success. It was even easy for us to mentor each of our clients individually. The hard part, the "cringe," came when we had to market what we do. For whatever reason, it never dawned on us that one of the partners should be good at marketing.

We need to make sure our *Precious Burning Desire* and our comforts and cringes line up. For instance, if you cringe at the thought of sitting in a room pouring over book after book, memorizing endless facts and your *Precious Burning Desire* is to be a brain surgeon you may have a disconnect. You'll either have to move your cringe to a comfort or find a different desire.

Commitment Leads to Consistency

If you are in sales of any type, there is a must-read book called "Influence: The Psychology of Persuasion" by Professor Robert C Cialdini. In this book, he talks about six different ways we are influenced to buy things. One of his observations will help us right here as we learn to dream big. He calls this "Commitment and Consistency."

In a nutshell, *commitment and consistency* says, once your conscious mind decides on a path of action (commitment) your subconscious mind will work to transform your lifestyle to this new commitment (consistency). This is really just the law of subconscious activity. The classic example of this is when you buy a lottery ticket. Most people, if they pick a number, tend to have a stronger feeling they will win AFTER they buy the ticket than before. This is because, after you make a commitment, you feel your universe must be consistent – if YOU picked the number to win, it MUST be a winner.

A problem you can run into when setting bigger than life dreams and *Precious Burning Desire*s is the conflict between what your subconscious wants to do to bring about your dream and what your conscious mind thinks you are capable of. In the next chapter, we will deal with this when we talk about *Exercise Your Faith Not Your Fear.*

I mentioned growing up poor and, at times, on the streets. Because of this, one of my comforts has been eating. Whenever food was around, I'd eat because (in my mind) I was afraid food would not always be available. Later, this would not be consistent with a *Precious Burning Desire* to be physically fit. Recently, I made this my BIG dream. Well, my personal trainer (who also happens to be one of the ***Life Changer 180 Mentors***, Christi) taught me to rewire my conscious mind with this affirmation: I don't diet, I eat according to my goals. Since working with Christi, I have lost 30 pounds.

If your comfort and your cringe line up with your dreams, then commitment to your dream leads to consistency in your quest.

So, one of the things we want to do as you are developing your *Precious Burning Desire*, is to make sure your vision of you and your vision of your dream line up. If you are reading this book with a big dream in mind, we want to make sure your core is lined up with your dream. If you want to develop a big dream while you are reading this book, we need to make sure this new dream lines up with the new you.

Yesterday, Today, Tomorrow

So far, we have looked at: The Conscious and the Subconscious, Comfort or Cringe, Commitment Leads to Consistency. There is just one other aspect of ourselves, our lives, we need to look at. I want you to spend the next several minutes (yes, it's OK to put the book down) reflecting on where you've been, where you are, and where you are headed if nothing changes.

This can be the most revealing (and, sometimes, the most painful) aspect of getting to our *Precious Burning Desire.* Ultimately, you will want to map out the path to get to your *Precious Burning Desire*, your ultimate, over-the-top dream. But to build that path, to build that map, you need to have a starting point. In Chapter IV we will deal with *Effective Planning*, making a detailed road map.

If I live in Baltimore, MD and I want to get to Miami, FL – it doesn't do me any good to ask someone living in Los Angeles, CA how they would get to Miami. I need to know how to get there from Baltimore. And, this supposes I even know I'm in Baltimore. And, that is what this section is all about – figuring out where you are right now.

To help us look at where we are and to look at the life path we would be on if the status quo stays the same, I want you to do an exercise. Look at where you were 7 years ago in 7 strategic areas of your life. Be honest with yourself – the more honest the better. Once you have looked at 7 years ago, do the same for today and then 7 years in the future. When you work on the future, look at it as if you just carry on from where you are now without any big goals. What I would like you to do is rank the individual areas of your life. "10" means things are or were or will be fantastic. "0" means "ain't nothin' happenin'." Take some notes. Here are the areas I would suggest you use:

Spiritual
Physical
Mental
Financial
Emotional
Social
Relationships

Once you finish this exercise, here is what I would suggest you do. As you go about your day, I want you to try an experiment. First, start thinking about your wildest dreams and what you've always wanted to accomplish in life. Some examples…

Gain wealth
Get in great physical shape
Learn a new language
Become a missionary
Be a better spouse
Be a better parent
Finish high school (when I was 19, this was a big deal)
Finish College

Then, I want you to fantasize about accomplishing these dreams for the next few days. If you go out to eat alone, just close your eyes and let yourself go. Don't hold back. Smile and dream! Think about all the emotions, sensations, feelings, associated with that.

If you find yourself eating with others, I want you to share what it would be like if you accomplished your *Precious Burning Desire*. I want you to smile while you are telling others. I want you to have fun with this. And, encourage them to tell you their dream. When they do, I want you to say, "Why not!? That sounds AMAZING!!" And just see how good it feels to enable someone to go for their deepest dreams.

SMART Goals

Having a *Precious Burning Desire* is a critical starting point. However, if you don't turn your *Precious Burning Desire* into actual goals, it will eventually just turn into a wish. You need to make sure your goals are meaningful. Your goals need to be SMART.

Specific. First, you need to make your goal specific. It's not enough to say, "I want to be able to talk to people about a saving knowledge of Jesus." You need to say, "I want to be able to speak to 7 people each week about Jesus and train 100 Christians each quarter to share their faith and I want to hit this goal within the next 12 months." It's not enough to say, "I want to be rich." You need to say, "I want to have a $5,000,000.00 net worth with $25,000 per month passive income within the next five years." It's not enough to say, "I want to lose weight." You need to say, "I want to lose 100 pounds of fat and increase my lean muscle mass by 10 pounds in the next six months." The more specific your SMART goal, the easier it will be to track and achieve.

Measurable. Not only should your goal be specific. It should also be measurable. Look, again, at the specific goals, above. Saying you want to be rich cannot be measured. What is rich? But, saying you want to have $5,000,000.00 in net worth - that is measurable.

Ambitious. Don't be shy or reserved when it comes to your desires and goals. Be ambitious. Make your goal something that is on the edge of "this can never happen." Dream big. God says, " I am the LORD thy God, which brought thee out of the land of Egypt: open thy mouth wide, and I will fill it." (Psalm 81:10) I think what He is saying here is we tend to not dream big enough. Stretch yourself and see what God can do.

Realistic. Your goal should be ambitious but realistic. You want to stretch to heights you have never reached. However, you don't want to set your goals so high they are impossible to reach. This is a fine line. There's a big difference between saying I want to lose 100 pounds in the next six months and I want to lose 100 pounds by next Tuesday. My suggestion would be, set your goal to whatever you have dreamed of accomplishing. Then, as you learn and plan (in later chapters) modify your goal if you need to.

Timely. A goal remains a wish until you put a time limit on it. You must tie your desire, your goal, to the calendar. By giving yourself a deadline you tend to work harder and stay focused. How soon do you want to start talking to 7 people each week? How quickly do you want to have five million dollars in net worth? When do you want to have that 100 pounds gone?

CASE STUDY I: EVANGELIST

Several years ago my wife, Cathy, and I were sitting in church. I don't recall what the sermon was about. I just know that I wanted to find out what God wanted me to do. This was a church that had alter calls at the end of the service. You could go to the front of the church and pray for guidance or talk to one of the pastors.

I went to the alter that day and prayed to God, "I'll do whatever you want me to do, You just have to show me what it is." God took me at my word.

Within about a week I developed a desire to tell others about Jesus and what He did for me. At this point in my life I had been a Christian for about 30 years. I could probably count on one hand the number of people I had talked to about Jesus. Now, after my prayer, I only wanted to tell people about Jesus and what He could do for them. God placed a *Precious Burning Desire* in my heart.

I really didn't know a lot about SMART goals at the time. But I did know enough to set some concrete objectives. I wanted to learn some sort of plan on how to talk to people about Jesus. Within a year, I wanted to be able to talk to an average of 7 people a week about their relationship with God. I would learn much later that my goals were nowhere near high enough for God. He had much bigger plans for me. He said, "Open wide." and I just kinda parted my lips a bit.

Case Study 2: Real Estate Investing

I started investing about 3 years before I started writing this book. At the time, we were running a non-profit ministry whose mission was to train pastors in third world countries to be better evangelists. This ministry was eventually replaced by the ***Lura B Walker Foundation*** and *Everyday Evangelism.* For the first few years of the ministry's existence, Cathy and I funded the majority of the trips with our personal savings. But, this could not last. We needed a better and growing source of financing. After much prayer and searching, we settled on real estate investing.

The most interesting aspect of this case study is that our *Precious Burning Desire* is not real estate investing. Real estate investing is just a means to an end. Our real passion here is the accumulation of vast sums of money in order to fund our evangelism efforts around the world.

By the time I started investing in real estate, I had a working knowledge of SMART goals. My goal for investing was to have a $5,000,000.00 net worth and $25,000.00 per month in passive income. I wanted to accomplish this within exactly five years of starting my investment career.

Case Study 3: Getting in Shape

My wife, Cathy, suggested I do a live experiment while writing this book. I need to lose, seriously, about 100 pounds. I am currently about 60-years-old. Up until about my 40th birthday, I was in very good shape - I was a professional martial artist and dancer. I then had shoulder surgery and, old story, it went downhill from there. I would gain some weight then lose a little weight. The gain was always just a tad higher than the loss. Over the last couple of years I have tried hard to lose the extra weight to no avail.

I take drugs for Type II Diabetes, Cholesterol, blood pressure and low thyroid. Numerous times I have played at getting back in shape. You would think that I would have done something about this a long time ago. But, life and work just stayed in the way and I never really had my heart in it. Now, I want it. No, I WANT IT! I want to be in shape. I am sick and tired of being sick and tired. I want to have energy to play with my grandchildren. I want to have energy to train in the martial arts with my wife and my oldest daughter. I want to prove to all of you that these seven steps really work! I have a *Precious Burning Desire* to get in shape.

My SMART goal for getting in shape seems very ambitious to me. But, I am modeling it after the show "Biggest Loser" and Dr Huizenga (the doctor behind the show). So, I believe the goal is also reasonable. I want to lose 100 pounds of fat and increase my lean muscle mass by 10 pounds by this summer - six months from now.

Exercises

1. Look at the things in life you want to accomplish. Make a list of the top few (no more than 10).

2. Pick one *Precious Burning Desire* from your list for the remainder of this book. Keep in mind your dream should line up with your comfort and cringes.

3. Make a list of the great benefits you and others will reap when you accomplish this desire.

4. Convert your desire to a SMART goal. Make sure to cover all five points. Write these down and, for now, put them in your wallet or purse. Read them every day.

II. Exercise Your Faith Not Your Fear

For God hath not given us the spirit of fear; but of power, and of love, and of a sound mind. (2 Timothy 1:7)

Once you have that *Precious Burning Desire*, the next step is to build the faith needed to accomplish your desire. It has been my experience that, the first time we try something new, it is very easy for fear to move in where faith should live. I believe fear and faith are actually different sides of the same coin. In any given situation we can be afraid something bad will happen or have faith something good will happen. Fear is just a faith in negative results.

Bob's Story

We drove by the house again. We looked at the roof, observed the trees in the front and back of the house. Cathy noticed the garage door was in disrepair. I noted the front door looked just as bad. Well, tomorrow the rubber hits the road. We would be going to our first tax deed auction to try to buy this particular house.

In the Case Study section of this chapter I will say, "Once I gained the knowledge and the plan to be successful, it was just a matter of execution." That sounds like such a sterile, simple statement. But, emotionally, it wasn't quite as sterile.

After doing all of our research on the house and driving by it, we were willing to pay up to $30,000 for it. Sitting here today typing this, it sounds like such a small amount of money. But, this was going to be the first house we bought as an investment property. $30,000 was a LOT of money to bet on something we had never done before.

James Smith had taught us how to buy properties at tax deed auctions. In these auctions, the county would try to sell off properties they had repossessed for delinquent property tax payments. The process, the steps, were pretty straight forward. The first thing we did was pick an area to invest in. Using criteria we had learned in our classes, we decided to invest in the south west part of Ohio. For the second step, we looked through the auction announcements to find the houses worth bidding on. We found the house we were going to try to buy. We did some analysis on the house using the internet. Then, we drove by the house to see it for ourselves.

Finally, the day arrived. It was auction time. I had absolutely *NO* faith in myself. I had never done this before. I had no idea how, exactly, it would work. But, I had faith in the process, the plan I had learned, and I had faith in God. I knew I was supposed to use real estate as a way to fund our ministry. We stood in the foyer of the court house. The auctioneer stood on the first step of the ornate, winding staircase. She first auctioned off all of the foreclosure homes. When she was finished, most of the buyers left. Now it was time for the tax deed auction. A couple of people bid on the house I was trying to get. But, it was my turn to win. We bought the house for $25,000 - $5,000 less than we were willing to pay.

Eventually, we put about $30,000 worth of repairs in the house and was able to sell it to a nice young lady with a child. She bought it on something called a Land Contract - simply put, we are the bank and she makes her mortgage payments to us. She has a very nice house to live in and we are making money on the house every month. The process worked! And, because it worked, we were one step closer to having faith in ourselves.

MOSES

Fear. Moses was a baby when he was adopted by Pharaoh's family. He was declared a son of Pharaoh. He was on the path to *BE* pharaoh. Then, at the age of 40, he saw a Hebrew and an Egyptian fighting. He intervened and killed the Egyptian. Moses had to flee his homeland. He eventually found himself in the wilderness working for a man named Jethro. He married one of Jethro's daughters and settled down. He had a new life and lived it for another 40 years. At the age of 80 his life changed forever.

At 80-years-old, Moses was tending the flocks on the back side of the desert and he came to the mountain of God, Mt Horeb. It was there he saw the burning bush. The Angel of the Lord appeared to him. God told Moses He would send Moses before Pharaoh to bring the children of Israel out of Egypt. But, Moses was so insecure in his own abilities, he told God, "No." He said, "I'm not an eloquent speaker. I am slow of tongue and ..." Moses was so insecure in his abilities that he actually argued with God.

Finally, the anger of God was kindled against Moses. He says to Moses, "Is not Aaron the Levite thy brother? I know that he can speak well." And, "He shall be thy spokesman unto the people."

Faith. Fortunately, Moses did not remain a man of little confidence. Nine times Moses stood before Pharaoh and said, "Let my people go." When the Red Sea stood on one side of the nation of Israel and the entire Egyptian army was bearing down on them from the other side, Moses rose to the occasion. Moses stretched out his hand across the sea and the waters parted.

At first, Moses just had faith in the process. He did what God said and went through the motions. He obviously didn't believe he could do what God said, he argued with God. But, he was willing to go through the motions. I think, as he saw the first miracle or two, he began to see that the process God laid out would work.

Next, Moses had faith in God. He saw the miracles of God time and time again. He learned, by the time he came to the Red Sea, that God would be faithful and fulfill His promises. He learned that he could trust anything God told him.

Finally, Moses had faith in himself. When Moses went to the mountain to receive the Ten Commandments, Aaron helped the Israelites form a golden calf to worship (not Aaron's brightest moment). When Moses came off the mountain and saw what the children of Israel were doing, He got angry. He threw down the tablets with the Ten

Commandments. He destroyed the calf and punished those that would not repent. He had become a decisive leader with the confidence to lead a nation.

Increasing Your Faith - In God

The ***7 PERFECT Steps to Success*** are universal laws. What I mean by that is, they can be used by anybody to become successful. In other words, it doesn't matter whether or not you believe in God, the laws still work. Just like gravity or electricity or any other physical law in the universe - they work for everyone. However, if you do have a right relationship with God, you have a leg up.

In the 37th Psalm, King David says, "Delight thyself also in the LORD; and He shall give thee the desires of thine heart." I don't think this means that, if you are happy in God, you will get whatever you want - that new Ferrari, a million dollars, a cruise around the world. Rather, I think it means, if you are in God's will, then He will place the proper desires in your heart. If you are in God's will, doing what He expects, then He will place desires in your heart for the things you should seek after. Basically, if you are in this position, you are the junior partner of a team consisting of the Creator of the universe and you - how can you lose?

But, how can you increase your faith in God? The first step is to make sure you have the right relationship with him. John 3:16 puts it very simply: "For God so loved the world that He gave His only begotten Son, that whosoever believes in Him should not perish but have everlasting life." See the Epilogue of this book for the four steps necessary to start your walk with God.

The next step is to understand God has already given you a measure of faith. The Apostle Paul tells us, "... according as God hath dealt to every man the measure of faith." The problem is, as we move further and further away from the moment we trusted in Christ, we can either move closer to God or further from Him. If you have moved closer to Him then you already have all the faith you need. If you have gotten to a point in your life where God seems distant then you just need to be re-introduced to your heavenly Father.

One aspect of faith is trust. You need to trust God. The best way to learn to trust someone is to get to know them. The best way to get to know God is to read His word, the Holy Bible, and talk to Him about all your dreams, desires, concerns and hopes. Talk to Him about everything. If you have been away from God and the Bible for a while, a great place to start is the Gospel of John - it's a great book for seeing how much God loved you by sending His Son to die for you. You can also see just how much Jesus depended on faith.

We will address this in a later chapter, but another great way to learn to have more faith in God is to hang out with Christians who are more mature than you. If you already attend a church where people seem close to God then pick out the great Christians and begin a friendship. If you are in a bad church or no church at all, find a church that is following God and look for that special person God is leading you to get to know.

Keep in mind, the Bible says, "For God hath not given us the spirit of fear; but of power, and of love, and of a sound mind."

Overcoming Your Fear

I won't say a lot about overcoming your fears. You will see in the next few pages (and as you implement the exercises at the end of the chapter) that the easiest way to overcome your fears is simply to increase your faith.

When someone tells me, "What's wrong? There's really nothing to be afraid of." Or, "Just plow through the fear." I just want to scream. Whether or not the fear is rational or whether or not the fear is well founded, it is STILL a fear. It is STILL real to the person experiencing it.

What I would like to do in this section is go through the academic part (the 3 steps to dealing with your fear with a couple of smaller exercises), then I want to give you a few practical exercises/assignments so you can practice.

Step #1: Is the Fear Even Worth Worrying About?

The first step is to decide if the fear is even a fear you need to worry about.

Some fears just don't matter. If you are afraid of killer sharks but you live in the mountains of Colorado, you can probably ignore that fear. If you are afraid of getting on a stage and speaking to large crowds but you are a stay-at-home mom with no need to be in front of large crowds, you can probably ignore that fear. But, if you have a fear of talking to strangers and you sell vacuum cleaners door-to-door you may have to deal with that fear. Try to come up with some fears you may have that just don't matter when it comes to fulfilling your *Precious Burning Desire.*

Some fears you should pay attention to. If you are

afraid of putting your hand into a roaring campfire you should probably hold on to that fear. If you are afraid of standing in the middle of the freeway during rush hour in a snow storm, I'd hang on to that fear. Can you name two or three fears you should keep?

Some fears you need to conquer. Now, there are some fears you probably need to deal with if you are going to step outside your comfort zone to achieve your *Precious Burning Desire*. For instance, if you have a service-based business you wish to expand across the country and you are afraid of working on the internet, you may need to overcome that fear.

If you are not sure what fears you may have that are keeping you from success, a great place to start is to look at your cringes. Let's do a quick review of comforts and cringes from the last chapter. Most of us are motivated to move towards comfort and to avoid, what I like to call, cringes. But, recall, what some people consider a comfort, others might consider a cringe.

In today's environment, you have to be computer savvy in order to work in the marketing arena. If you are afraid of computers, then your cringe about programming a marketing funnel is partly based on a fear. Not all of your cringes stem from fears but some of them probably will. Can you think of a couple of your cringes that may be based on fears you have?

Step #2: Figuring Out a Plan of Attack to Deal with Your Fear

When you have a handle on what fears you have that need to be addressed, the next step is figuring out how to deal with those fears. There are a lot of coaches and mentors out there who tell you to just face them and overcome them. I think these people are like the guy who only has a hammer and no other tools. When all you have is a hammer, every problem looks like a nail. Below, I list some ways I have dealt with my fears in the past to become successful. More than one may work for a given fear. Some may work for one type of fear and not another. And, you might even come up with some unique ways I haven't thought of.

Focus on the process and not the fear. Several years ago, Cathy and I took three of my daughters to Cancun. One day we went to the pyramids in Chichen Itza, Mexico. At the time, you could actually climb to the tops of the structures. We all climbed to the top of the highest pyramid. Once we got to the top one of my daughters realized she was deathly afraid of heights – to the point of being paralyzed. We had her sit at the top of the stairs. Cathy sat next to her and wrapped an arm around her. I got in front of her, had her stare into my eyes. Then, she scooted down one step at a time. In no time, we were all standing at the bottom of the pyramid. Sometimes, you have to put your focus on the process, put your faith in the process, and ignore the fears around you.

Focus on short term steps and not the bigger issue. I run a foundation (Lura B Walker Foundation) that trains Christians in evangelism – how to share their faith with others. For a lot of different reasons, many Christians are very scared when it comes to telling others about Jesus. The foundation teaches a simple 12 step course (called the *Everyday Evangelism Program*) for getting through the process of telling others how to get to heaven. Most Christians find focusing on the individual steps and not the entire witnessing encounter a great way to get through their fear of sharing. Sometimes, you just have to take it one step at a time.

Delegate and avoid. Are you pursuing your *Precious Burning Desire* with someone else? Perhaps the thing you fear, they find a breeze. I speak in front of crowds in the hundreds, if not thousands. I have written several books. Words are my bread and butter. But, I just cannot bring myself to make phone calls. I will actually pay my wife, Cathy, to make my phone calls for me. For whatever reason, I just won't make calls. Rather than deal directly with this silly fear, I have been able to delegate and, thereby, avoid the whole issue. Sometimes, if you fear something, you can get someone else to take on that problem – your cringe may be their comfort.

Compartmentalize and avoid. I was taught there is more than one way to skin a cat. If you are afraid to do something to accomplish your goal, is there another way to do it? When I wanted to get back in shape I was more than100 pounds overweight. I just couldn't bring myself to go to the gym. It was party embarrassment for what I had become and partly fear of what others would say. Fortunately, I was doing fairly well financially by this time. I set up a gym in my house where I could work out in private until I felt comfortable working out in public. Sometimes you can compartmentalize the fear and just go around it.

Find a buddy. If you can get someone to go on the journey with you, they can act as moral support. This especially helps if you are afraid to "be first" but can follow someone else. And, keep in mind, there is no rule that says you have to blaze a new trail to get to your *Precious Burning Desire*. Growing up on the beaches of Los Angeles, I had a friend who loved to swim in the ocean. However, if we ever went to somewhere new, he would be deathly afraid to go into the water. He had an irrational fear of what might be under the waves. Myself, or one of our other friends, would have to go in first. But, once someone else went in, you couldn't keep him out. Sometimes you can get a buddy to go first or "hold your hand" as you go.

Design small steps and celebrate your victories. Someone once said the best way to eat an elephant is one bite at a time. If your *Precious Burning Desire* is so large it literally scares you and you are frozen into inactivity, the best thing to do is break it up into much smaller steps. When I decided to get my college degree, you may recall, I picked physics as my major. At the time, I had absolutely no idea what physics was or what a degree in physics would entail. When I found out what I had to do to get the degree in physics, I almost backed out. But, I had made a commitment to myself to do it. I got the requirements and laid them out on the table. I worked through how to make it possible then worked on one semester at a time. I never picked my head up to see what was ahead of me. I just focused on the tasks at hand. And, surprise, one day I did look up and I was finished.

Face it and plow right through it – brute force. Like I mentioned above, this is the most common suggestion out there. And, when all else fails, it really does work. When I first started studying the martial arts there was a day I had to break my first board. The instructor told me to think past the board, aim past the obstacle. I was nervous and didn't listen to his instruction. When I hit the board, it felt like the board hit back. It hurt like the dickens. I tried again and, this time, I listened to the voice of experience. I concentrated past the board and past my fear. The board broke and I couldn't even tell I had hit it. Since then, I have broken up to five boards at once. I have even successfully punched through 10 inches of concrete. After I was taught how to think past the obstacle and plow right through, it became easy. There will be some fears you just have to conquer and beat into submission.

Over the past several years of mentoring, I have seen some fears pop up over and over again. Let me list these for you. If you see some that resonate, then you can know others have gone before you and dealt with them successfully. This means you can also deal with them successfully. I have grouped the fears in three areas where I do a lot of mentoring: entrepreneurs (people starting new businesses), fitness (people trying to get in shape), and spiritual (people trying to get closer to God).

Fear of…	Entrepreneur	Fitness	Spiritual
Failure	x	x	x
Success	x	x	x
Public Speaking	x		x
Ridicule	x	x	x
Ignorance	x	x	x
pulling the trigger	x	x	x
technology	x		
people		x	x
not being good enough	x	x	x
not knowing enough	x	x	x

Step #3: Moving Forward, Taking Action

Once you decide whether or not you even have to deal with a fear and you have decided on the proper way to deal with the fear, the only thing left is to execute. So far it has been pretty academic. But, when you actually have to "do something" then you find out if you really believe in the work around you have come up with.

In order to be able to move forward, I want to use two concepts: one from the next chapter and one from the last chapter:

Positive Affirmation. Positive affirmations are based on two laws of the mind we covered in the last chapter – The ***Law of Unconscious Activity*** (Any idea or thought you accept as true in your conscious mind will be accepted without question by your subconscious mind. And, your subconscious mind will immediately begin working to bring it into your reality.) and the ***Law of Concentration*** (Whatever you dwell on grows and expands in your life.). The positive affirmation I would like you to try as you are getting ready to tackle your fear is:

> "My *Precious Burning Desire* is SO big; I can accomplish ANYTHING!"

Now, this is a generic affirmation. Later, in the next chapter, we will come up with more specific ones.

The Law of Substitution. This law says your conscious mind can only hold one thought at a time and you can substitute one thought for another. You will design a plan to tackle the fear based on what strategy you chose. By concentrating on your affirmation and on the plan you built, your destruction of the fear almost becomes an academic exercise.

Time to Try Some Exercises

Pick a fear that is holding you back from a particular aspect of achieving your *Precious Burning Desire* (be as detailed as possible, only you will see this). Get a blank sheet of paper and write it down.

Keep in mind, faith and fear are opposite sides of the same coin. Faith is the belief (and feeling) something positive will happen. Fear is the belief (and feeling) something negative will happen. With this idea in mind, try to come up with one or two affirmations that are direct opposites to the feeling you automatically have with this fear.

It's now time to decide on a plan of attack to defeat this enemy. Look at the ways I have used to conquer fears in the past. Here is the list of my strategies:

- Focus on the process and not the fear
- Focus on short term steps and not the big picture
- Delegate and avoid
- Compartmentalize and avoid
- Find a buddy
- Design small steps and celebrate your victories
- Face it and plow right through – brute force

Write down, under your fear, the plan of attack you are going to use.

Once you have decided on the strategy you will use,

now you have to design your plan of attack. It could be as easy as listing the steps you need to take to move around the fear. It could be as simple as calling a friend and talking them into taking care of it. Whatever strategy you pick; however, you still need to lay out the steps and a time line – recall, a dream without a plan is just a wish. On your sheet of paper, you can develop your steps to beat this fear. Note, the last step is a ***celebration***. Make sure you don't forget this step!

Increasing Your Faith - In the Process

If you find that you have low to no self confidence in accomplishing your desire, you need to know two things. First, you are in good company - recall, Moses had no confidence, even after he was directed by God. Second, you CAN improve your confidence. But, it will take some work. We are going to do this in two steps. First, we are going to learn how to have faith in a process. Then, we are going to translate that into faith in ourselves.

The first step to increasing your faith in yourself is to increase your faith in a process. This is actually easier than you might think. There are already hundreds of processes that you have faith in. Some of the processes you probably have 100% faith in are:

walking
talking
biking
reading
writing
eating
standing

sitting
bathing
driving

I can hear you now - "Those are all simple, everyday tasks - they don't take any special talent." Tell that to a new baby. Each one of those processes (and you probably can think of many more in your life) had to be learned from scratch. You may not remember what it was like when you learned to walk but, if you have ever watched a baby try, it took a lot of trial and error. It wasn't easy. First, the baby learns to roll over and scoot. Then they learn to crawl. Eventually they learn to pull themselves up to stand. Next, you see them take a tentative first step. Before you know it, they are running around the house getting into everything.

In chapters 4 and 5 we are going to talk about learning what you need to know to reach your *Precious Burning Desire*. Then we are going to learn how to develop a plan to get to that desire. If you find it a challenge to have faith in yourself, you can take a small step by having faith in the process, in the plan, that you develop with the expert knowledge you will gain.

Increasing Your Faith - In Yourself

Most people find they have a lack of self-confidence because they have been told they are "not very bright." Or, maybe, you were told you "don't have what it takes." Or, maybe, it is self-imposed. Maybe you didn't do well in math or science and you think you are "not too bright." Well, I'm here to tell you that someone did not give you the whole picture. You are brighter than you think. In 1983, Howard Gardner wrote a book called, "Frames of Mind:

The Theory of Multiple Intelligences." In this landmark book, Dr. Gardner presented what he called the seven intelligences. Spend some time looking at this list. Look for the one or two areas you feel the most confident. Look for that one intelligence you really feel comfortable in. You can use this particular intelligence as a jumping off place to build faith in your abilities.

Here are the seven intelligences he presented:

Intelligence	**Occupation**	**Attributes**
Logical	Scientist Mathematician	ability to discern logical and numerical patterns
Linguistic	*Writer* *Journalist*	*strong usage of language, understanding rhythms and meaning of words*
Musical	Composer Musician	ability to produce and understand rhythm, pitch, and timbre of music
Spatial	*Navigator* *Artist*	*capacity to perceive and manipulate the visual-spatial world*
Bodily-kinesthetic	Athlete Dancer	ability to control one's body movements and handle objects
Interpersonal	*Manager* *Counselor*	*understanding the moods and motivations of others*
Intrapersonal	person with accurate self-knowledge	ability to access one's own feelings and use them to guide behaviors.

This is probably the hardest part for a lot of people - faith in yourself. If you have read my story in the Preface and the first part of chapter 1, you already know there was a point in my life where I had no self-confidence. When I went after my physics degree, I trusted in the processes. I had learned a few study habits during my 3 semesters at bible college that I would apply in my studies of physics. I prayed a LOT and asked God daily to guide me. It wasn't until the last year of my degree that I began to see I could make it. I began to get confidence in myself that comes from having faith that I could do it.

If you are still struggling with self-confidence and need some beginning baby steps while you are getting started, there are a few things you can do.

One technique I thought was silly until I tried it and it worked was what one of my mentors called, "fake it 'til you make it." He didn't mean to lie about who you are and what your capabilities are. What he meant was to act like you envision a confident person would act. Stand with your shoulders back and your head held high. Look people in the eyes when you talk to them (yes, it is hard the first time you do this but you CAN do it). Speak with a confident voice. Look for someone you know that is confident (but not cocky). See how they act. Try to emulate them.

While we are on the subject of people, there are some people you should avoid like the plaque. Someone once said, "If you want to see what you are like, look at the four people you hang out with the most." Do you know any people in your inner circle of friends who are always negative? If so, honestly, you need to not hang out with them. If you want to be successful, you MUST hang out with positive, successful people. I looked at the people I was hanging out with and found two people that were always (I mean ALWAYS) negative. You could say, "Wow, the sun is shining." And they would say, "Yep, looks like the crops will dry out now." I decided to minimize my exposure to them and, within a week or so, I could tell my outlook on life was changing.

In order to get to where you are today, you had to be

good at something. Are you a great organizer? Maybe you are good at getting a project off the ground. Do you have any trophies, no matter how old? Forget, for now, about your shortcomings, focus on your strengths. Make a list of what you are good at.

Finally, a great way to increase faith in yourself, is to count your blessings. One of the things Robin Strempek (the CEO of ***Life Changers 180***) does every night when she tucks her daughter in to bed is name a blessing. They each have to come up with one thing they are thankful for that day. It can be something as simple as her daughter saying, "I'm thankful for having my favorite desert tonight." Or, it can be as complex as Robin saying, "I am thankful we were able to help over 100 people to imagine a new dream today."

CASE STUDY 1: EVANGELIST

My faith in God is really what got me started here. I knew, beyond a shadow of a doubt, that my desire to reach the lost with the gospel of Jesus Christ was a God-given desire. This was a great motivator.

I didn't know how to talk to people about God. I didn't have a process to be confident in. I had no experience in telling people about Jesus. I didn't have any confidence in myself. But, my confidence in God was enough to get me started until I learned what I was doing. I stayed driven with this faith. It took me to great success.

CASE STUDY 2: REAL ESTATE INVESTING

I had gone to a motivational rally at about the time I

was looking for alternate sources of income for my ministry and funding for our overseas trips to work with pastors. There were about a dozen highly energetic and extremely motivated speakers on the stage. They were very good at convincing me I could do anything!

Because of this, by the time I decided to begin investing in real estate, I was convinced (absolute faith) I could do it. Once I gained the knowledge and the plan to be successful, it was just a matter of execution. Wrapped in the faith I could do it, I jumped in with both feet and never looked back.

Case Study 3: Getting in Shape

The amount of faith I started with in real estate was balanced with the amount of fear I started with in getting in shape. I have been heavy for over 20 years (almost 33% of my life). Though I have been very successful in almost every aspect of my life, my weight has not been one of those areas. I have a *Precious Burning Desire* to get in shape. But, over the years, I have lost faith in my ability to get there. On more than one occasion, I have told Cathy it is hopeless. I told her my body just won't cooperate anymore.

David (an international lawyer headquartered in Annapolis, MD) says, "When you have lost faith in yourself, you have to have faith in the process." In chapter 4 we will talk about gaining the knowledge to succeed. In chapter 5 we will talk about creating a plan to succeed. When you have lost faith in yourself, you need to have faith in this knowledge and the plan you build from that knowledge.

If you are like me, heavier than you know you should

be, then you are also probably an expert in all the diets that DON'T work. I can't tell you how many times I tried something new only to see it fail after a month, two months, maybe even a week. After I told Cathy I would take on the challenge to use the ***7 PERFECT Steps to Success*** to lose the weight I need to lose, we started watching old episodes of NBC's *The Biggest Loser.* The contestants on the show (if you haven't seen it) are really big. I could actually relate to them. And, guess what, they were actually losing their weight - some were losing 10 pounds a week. And, some of them actually kept it off.

I told Cathy, "With all these people losing so much weight, someone must be studying this." We found the doctor was working with the contestants – Dr. Huizenga. And, yes, he wrote a book about how they did it. I had completely lost faith in my ability to lose weight. But, after seeing the results on this TV show, I told myself I could have faith in the process until my faith in me is restored.

EXERCISES

1. Find something you have always wanted to do. Make it something easy to do - cook a new dish, learn a new exercise, or even how to work a DVD player. Find out the process and work at it until it is second nature.

2. Find something a little more complicated than the first exercise. Learn another process.

3. Find a quiet time every day for the next 3 weeks to read your Bible and pray. Maybe, play some worship music. Cathy has put some really great worship music together on www.YouTube.com – "Cathy's Favorite Worship Songs." Give yourself at least a half hour to get to know

your heavenly Father all over again.

4. If you are not already in a good church, explore the churches in your town every Sunday until you find one that uplifts you and makes you feel closer to God.

5. Find a mature Christian with a great positive attitude and make them your friend.

6. Practice acting confident. Find a confident person and emulate their confident mannerisms.

7. Examine the people you spend the most time with. If possible, try to minimize your contact with the negative people and increase your contact with the positive people.

8. List at least 20 things you are good at. Don't stop until you reach 20. If you have more, even better.

Organize for Success

Up to this point, we have built the foundation to make your desire a reality in "Going for the Gold." In the next three chapters, we will begin to shift that foundation to a certainty. We will talk about the first step in moving your desire from the mental to the physical with positive affirmations and visualization. We will talk about learning EVERYTHING you need to know to be successful in reaching your very own personal dream. Then, we will build a plan to get you from where you are to where you are meant to be – your *Precious Burning Desire.*

III. Repeat After Me

If any man among you seemeth to be wise in this world, let him become a fool, that he may be wise.(1 Corinthians 3:18)

In 1 Corinthians 3:18, above, the Apostle Paul says, "If any man among you seemeth to be wise in this world, let him become a fool, that he may be wise." Well, when I learned this step, I thought, "Boy, I hope this verse is true because I'm about to feel like a fool and hope to get wise." Well, it is very true. I was amazed at the impact of this step in the process.

Bob's Story

"Really? Does this positive affirmation stuff really work?" That was the question I asked myself when someone first introduced the concept to me.

"I don't know. They say it works." My mentor was not very much help.

I began to look for people who have actually used positive affirmations to make things happen. I met someone, John, who gave me a challenge.

John said, "Bob, you need to do an experiment to build your faith in affirmations. I want you to pick two thinks to see that you never see around you. Give yourself two days (48 hours) to see both of them. Once you pick the two items, I want you to look in the mirror each morning and describe the objects and say (out loud) that you will see them."

"Are there any rules?"

"You set the rules. Do you want to see the actual thing or will a picture of it do?"

I said, "Can I have different rules for each object?"

"Sure."

So, here's the experiment. First, I said I wanted to see a blue 1967 Mustang. Now, I live out in the country – Hanover, PA. I've seen some newer Mustangs but never my favorite. I said I had to see the actual Mustang. I was sure this would never happen. Second, I said I wanted to see yellow butterflies. It was the middle of winter so I said a picture would be good enough. I couldn't ever recall seeing yellow butterflies, real or pictured, so I was sure this wouldn't happen either.

I started my experiment at about 10PM on a Thursday night in the middle of winter. I had until 10PM on Saturday to complete my first step into affirmations.

I woke up Friday and walked to the mirror. I said, "In the next 48 hours I will see a 1967 blue Mustang and yellow butterflies."

First Item – 1967 blue Mustang. I had to drive downtown for lunch on Friday. On the way back, still in town, I saw it coming toward me, as big as life – a 1967 blue Mustang. I was so startled, I almost crashed. To make sure I wasn't seeing things, I turned around and followed it for about five minutes until the goose bumps died down.

Second Item – yellow butterflies. I didn't see anything on Friday. It was like 10° outside. So, I wasn't surprised that it would fail. I was happy with that. My experiment was 50/50 in the success department. I went to bed about 9PM on Saturday with still no yellow butterflies, an hour to go. I turned my computer on to watch a show while I settled down. I don't recall what the show was about, but I do recall the expression on Cathy's face when I yelled out, "Look! Yellow butterflies!" There on my computer screen was a wall covered in yellow butterflies.

I have used positive affirmations pretty religiously ever since.

JESUS

On the Sunday before the Crucifixion, Jesus rode into Jerusalem on a colt. After spending the day in Jerusalem, He retired to Bethany, on the other side of the Mount of Olives. The next morning, Monday, as Jesus and the disciples were walking back to Jerusalem, Jesus was hungry. He saw a fig tree with leaves and walked over to it to get a fig. But, it was barren.

Jesus then did something strange. **Jesus spoke to the tree**. He said, "No man eat fruit of thee hereafter forever." He spoke to the tree right in front of the disciples. The group then went on their way to Jerusalem.

When they arrived in Jerusalem they proceeded to the temple where Jesus overthrew the tables of the money changers. The disciples didn't think about the fig tree again.

The next day, Tuesday, as they walked from Bethany to Jerusalem, they came upon the fig tree. The disciples noted it was dried up from the roots and withered away. Peter said, with (I imagine) surprise in his voice, "Master, behold, the fig tree which thou cursed is withered away." Someone else in the group marveled at how fast it withered away - just the day before it was healthy.

Jesus said to them, "Verily I say unto you, **If ye have faith, and doubt not**, ye shall not only do this which is done to the fig tree, but also if **ye shall say unto this mountain, Be thou removed, and be thou cast into the sea; it shall be done**. And all things, whatsoever ye shall ask in prayer, believing, ye shall receive"

Jesus also said, "Have faith in God. For verily I say unto you, that **whosoever shall say** unto this mountain, 'Be thou removed,' and, 'Be thou cast into the sea;' and shall not doubt in his heart, but shall **believe that those things which he saith shall come to pass; he shall have whatsoever he saith**."

I can understand the fig tree withering up when Jesus told it to. After all, He is God. But Jesus told the disciples that we, too, can have that same power over nature. We can tell a fig tree to die and, if we believe what we say, it WILL die. Not only that, we can tell a mountain to move and, if we believe, then it will. That concept just blows my mind - we can control the world with our words, just like God did when He created the universe. Something to keep in mind, Jesus IS God but, He set aside His godly powers when He became a man. Everything He did, He did through the power of the Holy Spirit. In other words, He was our example – EVERYTHING He did, He expects us to be able to do!

My father-in-law tells a joke about moving mountains. A deacon of a church listened to the preacher preach on this passage. The preacher told the congregation, "You just have to believe and you can tell a mountain to move and it will move." The deacon went home and stood on his front porch. There was a small mountain between him and the ocean. He said to the mountain, "When I get up tomorrow morning, I want you to move to the other side of the house so that I can see the ocean from my porch." When he awoke the next morning, he went out to the porch to see how his experiment went. The mountain was still there. He whispered to the mountain under his breath, "I figured you'd still be there." You need words AND faith!

The Biblical Power of the Spoken Word

There are really two reasons why it is imperative that you verbalize your Precious Burning Desire. One is spiritual and the other is psychological. I first want to address the spiritual.

God tells us we are created in His image. Part of God's image is His ability to create through the spoken word. Though this aspect of our inheritance from God is not often addressed, it is critical to our success. Throughout the Bible, time and time again, there are examples of people speaking to nature and nature responding.

"And God said...". It all started roughly 6,000 years ago when God spoke the universe into existence. Eight times in six days the Bible records that "God said..." and things happened. I'm not sure why God chose to use the spoken word as His method of creating the universe. But I do know, when He did it, He set up a universal law which states what you say out loud has supernatural power. And, by supernatural, I mean above and beyond the natural and, to a large extent, in control of the natural. It may help to look at some historical examples of this universal law.

Isaac blesses Esau and Jacob. Jacob and Esau were twins of Isaac. But, as twins, they could not be more different. Esau loved to hunt, Jacob was a farmer. Esau was a hairy man, Jacob was smooth skinned. When Isaac was old it became time to give his blessings to his sons. As the oldest twin (by seconds), Esau was entitled to the better blessing. But Jacob made some venison for Isaac and, dressed as Esau (he even had fur on his arms to mimic Esau's body hair), he went in to see his father to get Esau's blessing.

Isaac blessed Jacob (thinking he was blessing Esau). He said, "God give thee of the dew of heaven, and the fatness of the earth, and plenty of corn and wine: Let people serve thee, and nations bow down to thee: be lord over thy brethren, and let thy mother's sons bow down to thee: cursed be every one that curseth thee, and blessed be he that blesseth thee."

When Esau found out what happened he wept bitterly. He had lost his blessing to his brother. Today, we would think, "Just take it back from Jacob and give it to Esau. After all, he took the blessing under false pretenses." But, they knew it didn't work that way. A man's word is his bond. Esau knew, once said, the spoken word cannot be taken back. He could not get the blessing now.

Moses striking the rock. This is, actually, a negative example. God had told Moses, "Take the rod, and gather thou the assembly together, thou, and Aaron thy brother, and **speak** ye unto the rock before their eyes; and it shall give forth his water." He commanded Moses to speak to the rock. But Moses hit the rock with his rod twice, instead. Because Moses did something physical to bring forth water instead of speaking like he was commanded, God would not let Moses enter the Promised Land.

Moses had led the Israelites out of Egypt. He had ruled them for 40 years. He wrote the first five books of the Bible. But, for this simple act of disobedience (he hit the rock instead of speaking to it), God forbade Moses from entering the Promised Land.

Joshua and stopping the sun. Joshua had taken over command of the Nation of Israel after Moses died. Under his command, the Nation of Israel had defeated Jericho and Ai. Now five kings of the Amorites were attacking an ally of Israel, the Gibeonites. And the Gibeonites asked Israel for help.

A battle ensued. The Amorites were on the run. God had sent great stones from heaven to kill the Amorites. And, as the Israelites were chasing them, Joshua said (in the sight of Israel), "Sun, stand thou still upon Gibeon; and thou, Moon, in the valley of Ajalon." And the sun stood still, and the moon stayed, until the people had beaten their enemies.

Joshua spoke to the sun and the moon and the entire earth stopped rotating.

David and Goliath. I talk a bit more about this event later in the book but, for now, I want to focus on what David said before he engaged Goliath. Just before David met Goliath in battle, David with a staff, a sling shot and five smooth stones and Goliath in full battle gear, David spoke to Goliath.

He said, "Thou comest to me with a sword, and with a spear, and with a shield: but I come to thee in the name of the LORD of hosts, the God of the armies of Israel, whom thou hast defied. This day will the LORD deliver thee into mine hand; and I will smite thee, and take thine head from thee; and I will give the carcasses of the host of the Philistines this day unto the fowls of the air, and to the wild beasts of the earth; that all the earth may know that there is a God in Israel. And all this assembly shall know that the LORD saveth not with sword and spear: for the battle is the LORD'S, and he will give you into our hands."

David spoke the pronouncement of Goliath's fate. And it was so.

Our salvation. In the book of Romans, the Apostle Paul tells us, "Whosoever shall **call** upon the name of the Lord shall be saved." He also says, "That if thou shalt ***confess with thy mouth*** the Lord Jesus, and shalt believe in thine heart that God hath raised him from the dead, thou shalt be saved." This last verse parallels what Jesus said about moving mountains, "... believe that those things which he saith shall come to pass; he shall have whatsoever he saith."

We need to pray, out loud, to God to cleanse us from our sins. And we must believe in our hearts that He will do this.

Jesus' command to speak to our mountains. We have already looked at the promise of Jesus that we have power over nature through our spoken word. An interesting Bible study would be looking up every place God tells us the importance of what we say and how it will have an impact on our future prosperity or poverty.

The Psychological Power of the Spoken Word

Not only is there a spiritual aspect to verbalizing your *Precious Burning Desire*, there is also a psychological reason.

In marketing, there is a technique that marries commitment with consistency (we talked a bit about this in chapter one). It is believed, if you will make a small commitment towards something (perhaps saying to a sales lady a particular dress would look good on you) then you are more apt to buy that dress so your world view stays consistent. Have you ever noticed lately cashiers are asking you for several pieces of data (name, zip code, other personal data) before they ask if you would like to be on their mailing list? They are trying to get you to make some commitments so you are more likely to stay consistent and agree to give them your email or home address.

Positive affirmations work the same way. Except, this time you are your own sales person. By verbally committing to your *Precious Burning Desire* you are making a commitment. And, because of your human nature, you will be more inclined to make consistent actions (some of them even unconsciously) to fulfill your desire.

You will find, as you start pursuing your *Precious Burning Desire*, you start to develop a faith you will achieve the dream in your heart. Remember, words are powerful. Recall the biblical examples, above. Words have power beyond our understanding.

POSITIVE AFFIRMATIONS – HOW TO MAKE THEM REALLY WORK

Enough "theory." It's time to actually put together your affirmations. What I would like to do is go over ten "rules" I use to build my affirmations. These are not hard and fast rules. Affirmations are as much an art as it is a science. I would suggest you start with the rules here. Then, as you see your affirmations starting to work, come up with your own set of rules.

A *little practice never hurt anyone.* This step is designed to help you build faith in yourself and in your ability to use positive affirmations. If the world of positive affirmations is new and unusual to you, do yourself a favor and pick some affirmations of current successes. For example…

If you already…	Your affirmation might be…
Lost 10 pounds	I am in shape
Have a job	I am gainfully employed
Graduated college	I am a college graduate
Made over $1,000,000	I am a millionaire
Gotten in shape	I am physically fit
Fixed your credit score	I have great credit

The point is, to make affirmations about something you have already accomplished. Why? Well, first, it builds confidence. Second, and maybe more important for later affirmations, it allows you to capture the emotional rush associated with success. Act like a child who just got an

"A" in a difficult subject. Be like a kid who got the BEST present for Christmas. We will use this in a couple of steps from now.

Keep It Simple. Now that you have practiced and have a little bit of the concept of affirmations, it's time to jump in the pool. But, let's not jump off the high dive. Let's go down to the shallow end and wade into the pool. Let's start with some simple affirmations to get you going. This is where I started – baby steps. Here are some examples of …

Some Simple Affirmations
I am happy
I am physically fit
I am rich

It's All About Attitude. Your affirmation needs emotion and passion. When you made the affirmation of previous successes, hopefully, you let the emotions of your success wash over you. When you build our affirmations, the more emotion you can put into it, the more your subconscious believes you. Try this with the affirmations in the previous step. If you do it in front of someone and they are not laughing, you are not putting enough emotion and passion into it.

Positive. When you make an affirmation, your mind cannot tell the difference between a negative and positive statement. It only knows to go after what you say. In other words, you can say, "I am not poor," or "I am rich." All your subconscious hears is "poor" or "rich." That is why you always hear people talk about positive affirmations. Everything you say (not just affirmations) should be said in positive language. Rewrite the following to be positive:

I am not poor
I am not sick
I am not a failure
I am not fat

There is power in the present. Keep in mind, you are using your conscious mind to rewire your subconscious mind. And, if you are like most of us, there is a lot of junk inside that you need to rewire. Because of this, we need to use every trick we can to strengthen your affirmations. After infusing the affirmation with emotion and making them positive, the next strongest thing you can do is declare the affirmation as in the NOW.

Simply put, instead of saying, "I will get in shape," you should say, "I am in shape."

Be YOU and not ME. You want to be yourself when you write your affirmations. You want your subconscious to believe your conscious mind believes what you are saying. If you say it the way I would, you take away some credibility. You need to put it in your own words.

WHAT not HOW. Your affirmations are a declaration of your ultimate goals. You don't need them to get bogged down in how they will come to pass. In the next two chapters we will deal with all of the *hows* to building your *Precious Burning Desire.* You don't need to worry about all of that when you are making your positive affirmations. You just need to declare your *Precious Burning Desire* will come to pass. When I was younger, there was a saying: KISS – Keep It Simple Silly. This is critical here.

Make affirmations about ANYTHING. Positive affirmations are about allowing your subconscious mind to work out the details on what you are trying to accomplish. Nothing is off limits. If there is something you want, make an affirmation.

A friend of the family was telling her grade school child about affirmations and vision boards (see the next section). Her son decided to make an affirmation about getting a hamster. Before the week was out, Snowflake became part of the family.

There is a lot in a little. I saw a posting on the internet (everything is on the internet) that listed "the 100 affirmations you need for your life" or something like that. I am from the other side of the equation. I think the fewer the affirmations, the more impact on your life.

Don't forget, you are not making up positive affirmations just to have a bunch of warm-fuzzy, touchy-feely platitudes that have no impact on your life. You are putting together part of a plan to reach whatever dream you have in your life. You need to stay laser focused on what you are doing.

With just a handful of positive affirmations, you can say them every day (or, several times a day) without getting burned out. You can say them every day and keep your energy and passion up. Imagine standing in front of a mirror everyday reciting 100 positive affirmations. I think I would last a day. Keep your affirmations tight and manageable.

Fantasy leads to Reality. Day dream about your affirmations. Roll them around in your head. Smile and just bask in the success. Positive affirmations are a good start. They are a great way for your conscious mind to push your subconscious mind into a new paradigm. But they are just a start. Throughout the day, when you find yourself day dreaming, try to day dream about your affirmations. Become obsessed, become laser focused.

SEE IT

As we move our *Precious Burning Desire* from the mental to the physical, another technique to make it real is a Vision Board. I find it really easy to verbalize my *Precious Burning Desire* for a week, maybe even two weeks. But, eventually, I forget. First I forget just one day. Then I'm good for a few days. Then I forget again. Pretty soon I am forgetting to verbalize my desire more times than I am remembering. Eventually, I'm not saying it at all.

A vision board can help you to remember to vocalize those desires. Cathy and I have our vision board set up in our bedroom. On the wall opposite our bed there are two doors. The one on the right leads to the bathroom. The left hand door leads to a closet. There is a four-foot-wide section of wall between these two doors. We have a large cork board hanging right there. When we get up in the morning it is staring right at us. When we go to the bathroom or get something out of the closet, we can't miss it.

We pin all of our dreams on this board. Sometimes it is words, sometimes a picture. All of the Case Studies I talk about in this book are represented on the board. The words or pictures we have to represent these desires (and all our others, for that matter) change every few weeks to keep them fresh.

In the 1956 film "The King and I" Yul Brynner's

character was fond of saying, "So let it be written, so let it be done." There is a lot of truth in those words.

Share It

Once you affirm daily the reality of your *Precious Burning Desire* and place it on a Vision Board to be before you every day, the next step is to tell others. It is a very powerful motivator when your relatives, friends and acquaintances know your desires and your dedication to achieving them. You work a whole lot harder.

As I write this paragraph I am sitting at a sandwich shop on Ft Detrick, MD. I just visited Cathy's office. I have been working on the "Getting in Shape" goal for 68 days now. Cathy's best friend at work, Becky, has known from the start what I was trying to do. Cathy wanted me to come in to show Becky my progress. Cathy and Becky were standing inside the front door as I walked in. Becky's jaw dropped when she saw me. This is the first time she has seen me since I started to prove the ***7 PERFECT Steps to Success*** can work even on my weight problems. In the last 68 days I have lost 42 pounds. - averaging over a half a pound every day. Not only was I extremely motivated over the last couple of months so as not to embarrass myself in front of Becky the first time she would see me (today), I am now even more motivated to finish strong so the next time she sees me I can declare victory.

Tell everyone who will listen what you intend to do. Don't be shy. If they will listen, you tell them with as much confidence as you can muster. Don't hold anything back. As you move forward and start to see progress (whether great or small) share with them the victories.

But What if The Affirmations DON'T Work?

If you are using positive affirmations, vision boards, and you are sharing with your friends, you should see an increase in your success. So, what if you don't see any success increase? In order to understand what might be going wrong, we need to go back to something we talked about in the first chapter.

Recall, in chapter 1, we talked about the Law of Subconscious Activity. This law states, "Any idea or thought you accept as true in your conscious mind will be accepted without question by your subconscious mind. And, your subconscious mind will immediately begin working to bring it into your reality." For most people, this helps positive affirmations work. But, there are two types of people who actually have this law work against them.

You'll never amount to anything. This is the group I was actually in. You may recall, I had a pretty rough childhood. Moving around from school to school, apartment to apartment, relative to relative I learned I was just an annoyance with a mom who didn't care. Most of the time we were being passed from relative to relative there were 3 of us. Imagine being the relative who had the honor of taking care of the 3 children from your dead-beat sister?

Solomon wrote in Proverbs 22:6, "Train up a child in the way he should go: and when he is old, he will not depart from it." Another way to look at this proverb is: "If you want to see why an adult acts the way they do, look at how they were treated as a child."

The only reason an affirmation doesn't work is if you already have another, stronger, counter affirmation in your head that you believe more. Whenever we have a student who does not respond well to positive affirmations, it ALWAYS goes back to something someone said to them as a child. And, it is usually something a loved one told them, someone they trusted and looked up to. Growing up, did anyone say these things to you:

> You'll never amount to anything.
> I can't believe how stupid you are.
> Shut up. Kids are meant to be seen and not heard.
> Go in the other room, I'm tired of looking at you.
> When I want your opinion, I'll beat it out of you.

These are words the people I trusted most, my parents, said over me. It took a LOT for me to overcome these affirmations and build a self-esteem that could take positive affirmations. When we talk to children, we need to be especially careful what we say to them. Children will rise (or lower) to our expectations.

When a low self-worth is beat into you day after day, eventually you begin to believe it. Eventually, the Law of Subconscious Activity takes its toll. Recall, what the law says is, if you believe something strongly enough (in your conscious mind), eventually your subconscious mind will work to bring it about. If you are told over and over again you are useless, eventually your conscious mind believes it and your subconscious mind begins to mold your universe around this reality.

Some people teach this as a lack of confidence. They teach, growing up in this type of environment, breeds a lack of confidence. I disagree. It's not a lack of confidence. Rather, it is great confidence in the wrong thing.

If this describes you, if you grew up in this type of environment, positive affirmations may not be able to break through your old belief system. If this is the case, you may need to seek more professional help at first. You may need to talk with a counselor or someone experienced in helping you to regain a normal sense of self-worth.

At the time of this writing, I am 59 years old. I have accomplished some amazing things in my life – things that would amaze the people I grew up with. But, I still struggle with my self-worth. It was so drilled into me as a child that I completely believed, until I got my degree in physics, I would never amount to anything. In chapter VII, we will talk about something called "Entrepreneurial Depression." As we will see in Chapter VII, this is a perfect place for all our insecurities to rear their ugly heads.

So, what do you do if this is your situation? It's pretty straight forward. You see, most people who read this book are going to brush over the preliminary exercises for Positive Affirmations. But, for people like you and me, these exercises are critical. We need to take small steps so we can build our confidence in the positive affirmations so we can prepare for the BIG steps.

Just prove it to me. This is the group that makes the *Show Me State* (Missouri) possible. It is the people who never believe anything on its face. They must see proof. And, however many years they have been alive, that is the number of years where they have seen proof contrary to the positive affirmations they are trying to invoke. The best thing this group of people can do is to go back to chapter 2 and model their initial positive affirmations around faith in God and faith in the process. Then, as they see the proof of their success, they can begin to modify their affirmations to revolve around their actual success.

If this is you, I want to suggest you do something different than positive affirmations. What I would like you to try is a visualization exercise.

There are just three steps, and you will need to finish *Chapter V: Effective Planning* to really be effective. But, here goes:

1. Think about what it will feel like when you achieve your *Precious Burning Desire.* Really revel in it. Spend several minutes just fantasizing about the end, about what YOU did to be successful.

2. While you hold on to that feeling, walk through the steps you took to get to that victory. Spend even more time here. Think through the major steps you set up to reach victory. Go through the steps like you are remembering how they were, not about how they will be. Imagine you are in a world where you have already accomplished the steps.

3. Now, go out and conquer the world. As you finish each step, go through this exercise again, dreaming about the steps left to accomplish as though you already have them under your feet.

If you are thinking, "Well, this won't work." Let me encourage you to put aside your "Just prove it to me" outlook and try to prove it to yourself. I'm so confident this will work for you, I want to ask you to email me when it does work: BobDudley@LifeChangers180.org.

Case Study 1: Evangelist

Over 30 years ago, when I had decided to get my bachelor's degree in Physics, I stumbled onto positive affirmations but never really made it an overt part of my success formula. When I was called to be an evangelist I didn't know a lot about the value of positive affirmations. However, I fell into the principles by accident. Once I recognized the desire to tell others about Jesus (witnessing) I started telling everyone I knew that I wanted to be an evangelist.

Within the first week I told Cathy that I was an evangelist. I wasn't sure how I was going to move forward or what my first steps should be. But, I knew, beyond a shadow of a doubt, that I was an evangelist. I told my daughters. I told people I worked with.

The only thing I did not do was put it on a vision board. But, I have fixed that oversight since then.

Case Study 2: Real Estate Investing

I did not make positive affirmations an overt part of my success formula until I started investing in real estate. Right away I employed the steps outlined in this chapter.

Every morning I look into the mirror and say, "I am a successful real estate investor." As I mentioned earlier, Cathy and I have built a vision board in our bedroom. It is on the wall at the foot of our bed, between the bathroom door and one of the closet doors. Every morning when I sit up in bed and every night before I lay down, it is before me. I have told everyone who will listen to me that I am a successful real estate investor.

Case Study 3: Getting in Shape

Since I started my "Getting in Shape" program while writing this book, there were no excuses for dropping the ball on positive affirmations. The day I finally agreed with my wife, Cathy, to make this part of the book, I came up with my affirmation statement. Every morning I look into the mirror and say, "I will weigh 195 pounds by this summer."

I found a picture of myself from when I was in my late 20s or early 30s and in great shape. I made a copy of this picture and placed it on my vision board. It is right next to the poster of the body builder. I pass by it about three or four times a day. When I stop noticing it (and it becomes part of the background) I will change the picture and put it on a different part of the board.

I started telling everyone I know that I am about to lose an incredible amount of weight. Every week I tell Cathy and my daughters how I am doing. I talk to my friends and family freely about my progress - both good and bad.

Exercises

1. Write your goal from the first chapter into a one sentence affirmation.

2. Build a vision board and hang it somewhere you can see it several times a day. Cork boards are good for this. You can buy a board at most office supply stores and department stores.

3. Find a picture (or, several pictures) that best represents your goal and put it on the board. As you grow and become comfortable with the ***7 PERFECT Steps to Success***, you will start to add other pictures to your vision board. Look at these pictures every time you pass the board.

4. Keep updating your pictures. If they stay the same they may become part of the background.

5. This week, tell at least two people (five people is even better) about your Precious Burning Desire.

IV. Firsthand Knowledge

The heart of the prudent getteth knowledge; and the ear of the wise seeketh knowledge. (Proverbs 18:15)

In *Chapter I: Precious Burning Desire*, we laid out our big dream and turned it into a goal. Then, in *Chapter II: Exercise Your Faith Not Your Fear*, we learned how to build our faith so we could achieve our dream, our goal. In *Chapter III: Repeat After Me*, we began the journey from having something inside of us we want to accomplish to bringing it outside. In this chapter, we are going to look at the practical aspects of reaching our goal. We are going to look at what knowledge base we need in order to be successful.

Bob's Story

While serving in the Air Force, I had the opportunity to be a Master Instructor at the United States Naval Academy in Annapolis, MD. When serving as an instructor at one of the military academies, Air Force officers are required to participate in academics, athletics and leadership development. Academics and athletics were easy - I was there to teach astronautical engineering and I already had a

4th degree black belt in Tae Kwon Do (and the academy had a Tae Kwon Do team that was in need of an OIC - Officer in Charge).

The leadership, that was a completely different story. There were only two venues for teaching leadership available to me. Most leadership was taught in the dormitories and not accessible to the academic staff. What was available were two different seamanship programs. There were, what the midshipmen called, the grey hulls. These were a group of boats that reminded me of the movie PT 109 or the TV show McHale's Navy. Also, there were 44-foot sloops - sailboats, to the uninitiated. I had to volunteer to be one of the officers teaching midshipmen on one of these boats. The problem was, up until this point, the only "boat" I had ever been on was a cruise ship – I mean, I was in the Air Force.

The first week of classes, I asked my students which one I should learn and get involved with. They laid it out in terms I could understand. They said, "If you want to learn about how to run a naval ship, you need to get involved with the grey hulls. If you want to have fun, you need to learn how to sail the 44 ft sloops." Easy decision - the next day I signed up for lessons on the sloops.

I spent the next year learning everything there was to sailing a 44-foot sail boat. I learned how to patch a sail, mend a rope, fix a toilet (excuse me, latrine) in the middle of the ocean. I learned how to patch a hole in the hull. I learned about celestial navigation and working at the helm. After a year of classes every afternoon followed by a few hours on the Chesapeake Bay every day, I was ready to teach young naval men and women.

The year I began teaching my midshipmen was very exciting. Myself and one other officer were to train eight midshipmen (six sophomores and two seniors) on the Valiant, an Audacious class sloop. We started with several weeks of sailing on the Chesapeake Bay getting to know each person's strengths and weaknesses. We worked on all the skills needed for the "final exam" - a 15 day trip to Bermuda and back.

The week before we were to head to Bermuda, we did a shakedown cruise around the Delmarva peninsula. This was a three day trip with about a day of actual "out to sea" time. It was a very sedate trip. We even spent a few hours swimming in the Atlantic Ocean.

Finally, the day came to load five days of supplies into what started to look like a very small boat. We would sail with two crews. On the way out, each officer would be the crew captain of four midshipmen who would work the boat. On the way back, the officers would become strictly safety officers and the seniors would run the crews.

The morning we were to leave, there were reports of storms passing through. It began to sprinkle a bit as we left the dock along the Severn River and headed out to the Chesapeake Bay. It took 24 hours to make it to the mouth of the bay. By the time we hit the Atlantic Ocean everyone on board was soaked to the bone and would stay that way the entire trip to Bermuda. As a matter of fact, the storms turned into raging tropical storms. And having a year of firsthand knowledge was about to pay off.

It takes about four days to sail from the mouth of the Chesapeake to Bermuda. The rain and storms were a nuisance the first day and a half. Then, the storms turned into tropical storms. I knew we were in trouble when we were sitting in the trough between two swells and the swells were higher than the 62 ft mast. We rode up one of the swells and it felt like we would fall over backwards. My crew was on deck - everyone tied to something on the boat. The other crew was trying to sleep, tied up, in their bunks below deck. The winds had kicked up enough to rip our storm sail. There were, actually, four sloops on their way to Bermuda. On one of them, because of the winds and waves, one of the crew had to be air lifted to an aircraft carrier due to extreme sea sickness.

Though I had never been in a storm of this magnitude, I had over 1,000 hours at the helm of this exact boat. I knew it like the back of my hand. For the next 24 hours I spent half the time keeping us from capsizing and half the time tied in my bunk praying. I believe, to this day, if I had not had the hours behind the helm that I did, I would not be here writing these words. Nothing can replace the experience and confidence that comes with firsthand knowledge.

DAVID

A lot of people know the story of David and Goliath. Goliath was a 9 1/2-foot-tall giant of a man that challenged the armies of Israel. If he won a battle between himself and an Israeli champion, then the victory would go to the Philistines. If the Israeli won, the victory would go to the Israelites.

All the army of Israel was afraid to fight Goliath. Nevertheless, the shepherd boy, David, was not afraid. David said, to the soldiers who told him about Goliath,

"Who is this uncircumcised Philistine, that he should defy the armies of the living God?"

He agreed to fight the giant and fight him with only a staff and a sling shot. As David approached Goliath he said, " Thou comest to me with a sword, and with a spear, and with a shield: but I come to thee in the name of the LORD of hosts, the God of the armies of Israel, whom thou hast defied. This day will the LORD deliver thee into mine hand."

David ran towards Goliath. And, as he ran, he reached into his bag to pull out one smooth stone. He fixed it in his sling and hit Goliath in the forehead. Goliath fell over, dead.

But, how did David know he could defeat the giant? When David went before King Saul to accept Goliath's challenge, the king placed his armor on David. David took it off and said, "I cannot go with these; for I have not proved them." He had no firsthand knowledge of the king's armor and how it worked. Instead, he decided to use a sling shot and five smooth stones. Why? Because he had firsthand knowledge of how to use them and he knew they would work. As a shepherd, he had already slain a lion and a bear with the sling shot.

So, What Do I Need to Know?

Sun Tzu was a military genius who lived around 600BC. His book, The Art of War, is studied by military strategists all over the world. Something he said will really help us here to figure out, exactly, what we need to know in order to be successful in achieving our dreams.

"To be victorious in battle, know your enemy, know yourself, and know your environment." Sun Tzu

Let's use this as an outline to see what we need to know to guarantee success when reaching our dreams. We need to know our goal, know ourselves, and know the environment we and our goal live in.

Know Your Goal

Here is a chance to really hammer out how your dream looks in the real world and the skill sets you need to reach it. If your dream is to own your own martial arts studio, what do you need to know besides how to break five boards with a side kick? If you want to lose a lot of weight and get fit, what do you need to know about nutrition, about exercise (both aerobic and anaerobic), about proper water consumption and sleep? The first chapter of this book, *Precious Burning Desire*, is about understanding your goal. You really need to have a handle on what this desire is and how it translates into a goal in order to see your dream become a reality. And, if you followed the advice and steps in Chapter I, you are well on your way!

Know Yourself

In chapter one (*Precious Burning Desire*) we talked a little about making sure your comforts and cringes line up with your big dream. In *Chapter II: Exercise Your Faith Not Your Fear*, we went even deeper in getting the confidence you need to reach your dream. We are going to spend even more time on "knowing yourself" in the rest of this chapter.

Know Your Environment

Really what we are looking at here are the external factors that will influence the journey to your goal. We'll spend some time on this in *Chapter VII: Tenacious Persistence* when we spend some time on the Success Curve. Make sure you stay until the end of the book. There are some very important lessons in that chapter. Lessons that will serve you well as you venture out into the world to see your dream become a reality.

GAINING BASIC KNOWLEDGE

There is a learning pyramid out there that is very controversial. Some people in academics just love it, others hate it. I want to take a few minutes to look at it in preparation for this section. I will let you decide if you are a fan of the pyramid.

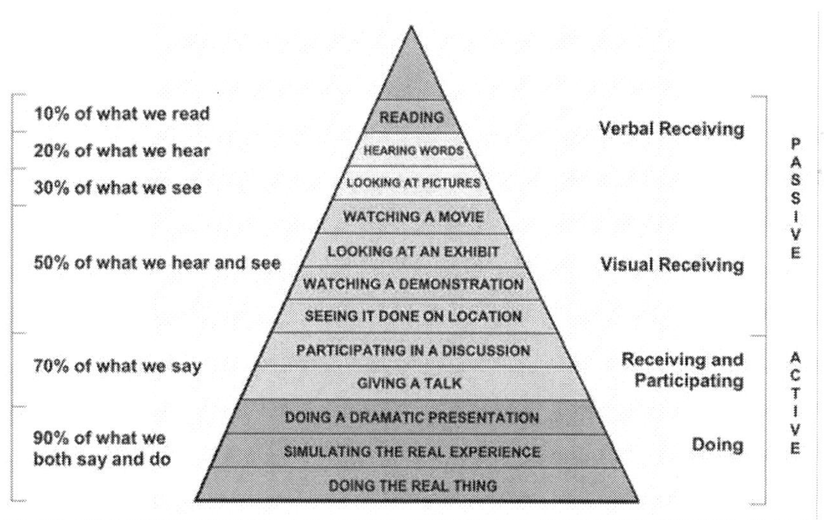

The people who are not champions of this pyramid usually fuss over the accuracies of the percentages. Let's put that aside. I think everyone can agree that the trends are accurate. What I would like to do is just point out the logic of the pyramid. Let's look it over.

One of the main points to get from the pyramid is, we learn and retain a whole lot more information when we learn actively instead of passively. And, it really doesn't matter what your learning style is. It doesn't matter if you learn by seeing, hearing, or touching. You can do any of these in a passive or active mode.

But, even beyond that, I think it is important to note all types of education can be useful. Especially, if you use them in a synergistic manner – putting them all together. When we first put ***Life Changers 180*** together, the idea was to optimize education to maximize the effect of all types of education for all types of learning styles.

Okay, with that as a background, first things first. Too many people come up with a great Precious Burning Desire then they just charge ahead, figuring they would learn what they need on the fly. Or, even worse, they think they know everything they need to be a success. At best, they wade through hard lesson after hard lesson as they blaze a trail into unknown territory. At worse, they get bogged down right away and frustration sets in to the point they quit.

A better approach would be to learn from those who have blazed the trail before you. No matter what your dream is, someone has done something similar enough that you can learn most of what you need from them. There are really just four ways to learn:

Study on your own
Take a class

Work with a coach
Work with a mentor

There are advantages and disadvantages for each of these. Let's take a moment to talk about each of these but, since most of us are very familiar with the first two, I'd like to spend most of this chapter talking about the last two. And, in particular, I will spend most of that time talking about mentors.

Study on your own. Whether your dream is to get fit, start a company or change the world, if you have gotten this far in the book then you are probably a self-starter. And, one of the characteristics of a self-starter (and, I'm speaking from personal experience) is you want to do everything yourself. This is a good start and can easily lead you to understand where the gaps are in your knowledge base. But, it's hard to figure out what knowledge is important/critical and what is just nice to know. You need to balance the ability to build your knowledge base fast with the inability (usually) to know what is critical knowledge and what is just nice to know.

Take a class. If you are not the completely "do it yourself" type person (or, you are but you need more data) the next logical step is to take a class. The advantage to taking a class or course is you get an instructor who (hopefully) knows what he or she is talking about and they know what to emphasize for the student. The downside to a class is, they tend to be more theory than practical application. My wife, Cathy, got an MBA with a concentration in marketing from a prestigious university (you would recognize the name). Her biggest comment when we started a company after she graduated, "I have absolutely no idea how to market this, or anything else for that matter."

Work with a coach. Basically, a coach is very task oriented. Their focus is to teach you, one-on-one, how to perform the tasks you need to accomplish to reach your dream. Your coach will help you to find your brilliance. They will work with you to develop the skill set you need to cross the finish line. They will be your accountabili-buddy – in other words, they will hold you accountable as you work through the steps you will put together in the next chapter. And, they will be there to guide you through the steps so you don't get lost in the weeds.

In 2013, Forbes Magazine published (online) "5 Things to Look for When Choosing an Executive Coach." Actually, the advice Erika Anderson gives in the article is great for anyone trying to find a coach. Here is my take on what you should look for in a coach in any walk of life:

1. They KNOW the process they are coaching. The job of a coach is to teach a skill set you can use in whatever venue you have hired the coach. They MUST be experts in that area. I recall someone telling me about a particular college professor. They said he is sooooo smart no one can understand him. If your coach is "so smart" no one can understand him or her, you need a new coach. If they own the material they can teach the material.

2. They look for your blind spots. A good coach will talk to your peers to find out their perspective on what you need to work on. We all have blind spots about our short comings. A good coach will talk to the people who know you best in the venue you are getting

coaching for. One area I have a big blind spot is in my writing. This book you are holding has been looked at by at least a dozen people before I sent it to the publisher. Once I write something, I can only see it in my head the way it is supposed to be (grammatically). I read right over any grammar mistakes I have made. Sometimes, when my editor points out a particularly glaring mistake, I'll go back to the original manuscript to look because I almost don't believe her.

3. They have a useful and relevant skill set. This is similar to #1, above. What I am looking for here is, they don't just have a head knowledge of what you are looking for. They actually have done it. When Cathy and I went to seminary, we were looking to work as evangelists after graduation. So, we were very skilled by this time in personal evangelism (talking to people one-on-one about God). We had to take a class on personal evangelism while we were in seminary. It was obvious after the first day of class that the professor had a lot of head knowledge about talking to non-Christians about Jesus, but he had never actually done it. By the third time we met as a class, all the students were looking to Cathy and I to validate everything he said.

4. They know how to keep their mouth shut. What I mean by this is, they will not betray anything you confide in them during your training. You need to know you can share with them your strengths AND your weaknesses. You don't want them telling everyone around you about private things you shared with them.

5. They have a proven track record of success. Not to beat a dead horse but, I really want someone to coach me

who really is doing whatever I am getting coaching in. And, I don't only want them to be doing it, I want them to be measurably good at it. When I got out of the army I had already earned a black belt in Taekwondo and competed successfully in international tournaments. Before I started my chain of martial arts studios, I looked for more training. I went through about 5 or 6 studios looking for people who not only could teach martial arts, but they actually knew what they were doing – they were good at their particular martial art.

As you go through this list of five things to look for in a coach, the list is fairly obvious. But, keep the list close when you are shopping. Don't just fall for the first nice, flashy coach you see, but interview them. Make sure they are a good fit for you and your goals.

Work with a mentor. A mentor is different than a coach. A mentor is almost a spiritual guide. Their job is to work on the inner you and to guide you to realizing your dreams through bringing out the best you there is.

We talked about picking a coach. What about a mentor? What should you look at when picking a mentor? Here are the four things I look for:

1. Can I respect the person? Here I am looking for two things, really. I want to know if they are someone who I think is an expert in the area I want to be successful in. Do they really get it and can they help me get it, also? The other thing I want to know is, are they someone who I can let inside? Can I let them see my most personal aspirations? Keep in mind, a mentor helps change the inside, they help you turn you into someone who can easily achieve your *Precious Burning Desire.*

2. Is this person respected in their field? Just because you like them and feel a connection, does not mean they are right for your particular dream. You need to make sure they are respected in their field. You need to make sure they understand where you want to go so they can really help you get there.

3. Can I work with this person? With a coach, you are learning certain external skill sets, tools, to get you to your goal, your dream. With a mentor, you are letting them inside so they can align your conscious and sub-conscious to your dream. This is a much more intimate arrangement than your coach. You need to make sure you can work with your mentor. There is a possibility they will have to lead you through some realizations that are painful. Make sure you can live through those moments with this person.

4. Do I think this person can help me reach my *Precious Burning Desire*? This really encompasses the whole package, everything we've talked about in the first three things I look for. Do you really think they are the person who can transform you into the superhero lurking inside of you?

What is the Best Approach?

As I alluded to earlier, the best approach is to put these four together. When pursuing your *Precious Burning Desire* you need to maximize your learning by putting all four learning methods together: study on your own, take a class, work with a coach, and work with a mentor. And, the best of all worlds, is to find all of those wrapped up in one place.

We tried to put this together when we formed ***Life Changers 180***. The process goes something like this:

1. When you sign up with ***Life Changers 180***, the first thing you get is a home study course called *Ignite Your Life* and a ticket to attend the 2-day live event of Ignite Your Life. In this course, you dig deep in the first two PERFECT steps to success. You learn how to dream big and have faith to accomplish your dream. Doing the home study course and the live event allows you to study on your own and take a class.

2. The next step in ***Life Changers 180*** is to round out the next five PERFECT steps to success. You will go through the home study version of Ignite the World. You will also attend the 3-day live event of Ignite the World. The last afternoon of the live event, you will get to spend a few hours in a group mentoring session where you will meet and interact with our Life Changers – these are trainers/coaches/mentors specially trained to guide you to success in your dream.

3. Once you have completed Ignite Your Life and Ignite the World, you are ready to work with your coach and your mentor. In ***Life Changers 180***, they are the same person – Life Changers. We have found combining a coach and mentor into one person helps accelerate your learning process and brings you closer to your Precious Burning Desire much faster.

Now, I'm not saying you have to join ***Life Changers 180*** to be successful. But, I would suggest you find an organization similar to it, if you want the best chance of success.

Case Study 1: Evangelist

When I first felt the drive to be an evangelist I decided to move forward with what I thought an evangelist did. Cathy and I would go to the docks in Annapolis, MD to try to talk to people about Jesus. I was going to witness to them and invite them to accept Christ (and become a Christian). Boy, was that a disaster. I had no idea what I was doing.

I had the determination but no education. A friend of mine (Dr. David Wood) says, "Inspiration without education leads to frustration." Was he ever right. For six months I would drag Cathy to the docks, or some other place where people would hang out, and we would walk around for an hour never talking to anyone.

It finally dawned on me there should be some sort of course you could take to learn how to do this. I found a class at a church about an hour from our house. The course was called *Soul Winners' Club*. I finally learned a plan and it changed my whole life. I now knew how to approach people in a loving manner. I learned how to get onto the subject of spiritual things. I could gently show people their need for Jesus and how they could make that decision to put their faith in Him to get them to heaven.

Case Study 2: Real Estate Investing

When we had settled on real estate investing as a means to secure the funds to do our evangelism work, we were a complete blank slate. We knew absolutely nothing about buying real estate as an investment. We took several courses on investing and eventually settled in with the *Rich*

Dad Education Company (Robert and Kim Kiyosaki).

The *Rich Dad Education Company* gave us a great foundational knowledge of the real estate investment world. Through their classes and mentors, we were able to gain the knowledge we needed to achieve the goals we set out for ourselves.

Case Study 3: Getting in Shape

If you are like me, way over weight and an expert at all the diets that DON'T work, then I want to tell you there is hope. I was an expert at getting in shape when I was in my 20's. I was even pretty good at getting in shape for someone in their 30's. But, wow, I sure had no clue how to tell someone in their 50's and older (yeah, I'm talking about me) to get in shape.

I had the self-taught knowledge. I even had taken a few classes on fitness. But, at this time in my life, I am in a whole new ball game. So, I brought in a coach/mentor – Christi. She made all the difference in the world. She was an expert in getting anyone in shape – even me.

Exercises

1. Write down you *Precious Burning Desire.*

2. Write down the things you already know that will help you reach your dream.

3. Make a list of gaps you see in your education. (you won't know all of them but write down the ones you do know)

4. Make an education plan to fill in the gaps. Decide what gaps are best served in the four different education venues:

   Study on your own
   Take a class
   Work with a coach
   Work with a mentor

V. Effective Planning

Go to the ant, thou sluggard; consider her ways, and be wise: Which having no guide, overseer, or ruler, Provideth her meat in the summer, and gathereth her food in the harvest. (Proverbs 6:6-8)

Earlier, we said a dream without a goal is just a wish. Actually, the same can be said of a goal without an effective plan. If our dreams were easy to realize, we would have accomplished them long ago. We need a good plan to guide us, especially during the difficult times.

Bob's Story

We bowed to the head referee then to each other. The ring ref put his hand between us and watched as we got into our fighting stances. I noticed my opponent's stance as I waited for the ref to announce the beginning of our first round. He stood with his left leg forward (standard) while I had my right leg forward (like a south paw). He stood slightly facing forward, an aggressive stance used for offense and allowing him to use his back leg easier. His arms were hanging, relaxed, by his sides – a normal stance in Tae Kwon Do tournaments. On the other hand, I stood with my back foot exactly behind my front foot, slightly on the balls of my feet for quick reaction but better for defense. My hands were up like a boxer.

The ref yelled in Korean then pulled his hand away. Immediately, my opponent threw a roundhouse kick to my head with his rear leg. This was a typical attack; one I have seen hundreds of times. As his kick came speeding towards me, I deflected it with my right forearm as I jumped into the air and spun counter-clockwise so that my rear leg came around in a back spinning side kick. My foot followed his leg back as he retracted. Almost as if my foot was pulled by his leg. I felt my heel connect with his rib cage – a forgone conclusion. My opponent flew out of the ring, a surprised look on his face, replacing the look of confidence he had when we first saw each other.

We faced off a second time. The ref, a second time, pulled his hand away from between us. My opponent tried to close the distance between us with a boxer's shuffle. I felt more than saw, the subtle shift of weight as he tried to raise his rear leg for a kick. I raised my right leg, my front leg, while shuffling in on my back leg. My side kick planted right into the same place I had hit him just seconds ago. He fell to the ground as his upper body stopped while his lower body tried to keep moving forward.

We faced off one last time. The ref, one last time, removed his hand from between us. This time my opponent shuffled in and tried a crescent kick to my head using his front leg. It was a simple matter to lean my body back to let the kick pass harmlessly in front of my face. As his foot found the ground, I spun around with a back-spinning hook kick. I connected with his jaw and he hit the floor like a sack of potatoes. Ten seconds later the ref declared the fight over, win by a knock out.

Did I win because I was faster than him? No. Did I win because I had better technique? No. I won simply because I had an effective plan and I knew how to execute that plan. I had planned and practiced my plan hundreds of times. Each thing my opponent did, I had one very effective counter for it. No matter what he did, I would know, by second nature, the one thing I would do to counter. I was so dialed in to my plan, the outcome was inevitable. My plans were so precise that my stance was pre-determined, how I held my hands, even down to the way I looked at him and concentrated on his center of gravity. There was never a moment where I had to guess what I was to do next. I could almost relax and enjoy the show.

JOSEPH

Through a long and arduous path, Joseph became Pharaoh's right hand man. The last step of this promotion came from prison. Pharaoh had two dreams. Basically, the first dream was about seven fat cows and the seven lean cows that ate the fat cows. The second dream was similar. It was about seven full ears of corn that were eaten by seven thin ears of corn.

None of Pharaoh's counselors could interpret the dreams. But Pharaoh's butler recalled a man in prison who interpreted the butler's dream. His name was Joseph. Pharaoh summoned Joseph to the palace. Joseph was able to tell Pharaoh there would be seven years of bounty followed by seven years of famine.

Joseph told Pharaoh he needed to appoint a discreet and wise man to oversee Egypt's economy for the next fourteen years. Then Joseph laid out his plan. Joseph explained how much food should be saved during the famine, he laid out how and where the grain should be stored. His plan was very comprehensive. Pharaoh was so impressed that he put Joseph in charge.

And, because Joseph had a plan and followed his plan, not only was Egypt saved, but Joseph was also able to save his family and be reunited with his family.

WHY DO I NEED A PLAN?

"Why do I need a plan?" That's what the young man asked me when we first met to start his mentorship. He was one of the first people I had ever mentored and all I could think to say was, "Um, because…" Well, we did build his plan and he did become successful. When I got home I decided I needed a good answer the next time someone asks me that question. So, let me share with you six reasons why we need a plan.

To Stay Focused

Life happens. I found, when I start a new project (especially at the beginning), life really gets in the way of my plans. If I want to get in shape, everybody and their brother wants to have lunch with me. If I want to start a new business, there always seems to be an emergency in one of my older businesses.

In this chapter, we are going to work on your strategic (long term) plan and your tactical (short term) plan. The strategic plan really helps keep the big picture focus. It allows you to see the end game. The tactical plan helps with the day-to-day management of your dream quest. With your tactical plan, you know what is expected of you each day.

I find the tactical plan is what I really need to keep my focus on. Every morning when I get up, I spend a few minutes thinking about what is on my tactical plan for the day. I write down some notes and a list of must-do's. Then, I hit the ground running. I know I MUST get everything on that list done to count it a successful day.

To Give Direction

In the introduction to this chapter, I described one of my fights when I was very active in martial arts. The first thing my opponent did was to try to hit me in the head with a roundhouse kick using his rear leg. There are, off the top of my head, about ten different ways to react to that type of attack. If I waited until he threw the technique to decided how I should react, the story would have ended quite differently.

Having a plan gave me singleness of purpose, it gave me one thing to do for everything he could do, it allowed me to stay on track and easily win. The plan I developed in the gym served me well in the ring.

Not only does a good plan keep you focused, it gives you direction. I find this very comforting. During a relaxed time, I was able to write out my plan so that, when things got tense, I didn't have to think about what to do. I just followed the plan.

To Have Effortless Decisions

This goes hand-in-hand with the last reason – To Give Direction. When you have a plan already laid out, decisions become effortless. I have found, and not just in the ring, having most of my decisions already mapped out really makes life a whole lot easier.

It has been my experience, when I don't have my decisions laid out ahead of time, I tend to continually second guess myself when I need to decide something. And, in the heat of the moment, I may forget some important aspect of the overall plan that is ruined because of the spur of the moment decision I made.

To Communicate to Others

This is probably one of the least thought about advantages to having a plan. But, if your *Precious Burning Desire* involves others, it is critical to have a plan to present to them. You may need to show your entire plan (to investors or business partners) or part of your plan (to employees or others you may need to delegate to).

Whenever I visit a bank or investor to ask them to put money into one of my companies, I bring a binder with several important documents – basically, EVERYTHING a banker could ever ask me about. I have my credit scores, photocopies of my driver's license. I have tax returns for both the particular company and my own returns. And, most importantly, I have a very detailed business plan (strategic plan). I want the loan officer or the investor to know that I have my act together.

To Get Little Bites

This one is BIG. And, speaking of big, how do you eat an elephant? One bite at a time. The advantage of having a *Precious Burning Desire* is it really helps you overcome obstacles that would stop others. Your big dream gives you a big "why." And, the bigger the why, the easier the try – in other words, the more your dream fills your heart, the easier it is to overcome anything in your way..

But, some people find having a big dream a little intimidating. As a matter of fact, Amy Cuddy (a Harvard psychologist) believes people have more success if they pick small goals – just down the block.

Having a good, detailed plan allows you the best of both worlds. You have your *Precious Burning Desire* to look forward to. But, at the same time, you have small monthly, weekly, or daily goals to hit. You get to eat that dream one bite at a time.

To Measure Progress

Another comforting aspect of a great plan, is the ability to measure your progress. Without a plan, it is hard to judge how well you are moving toward your *Precious Burning Desire.* I like to have my major milestones laid out in my strategic plan. Then, I like to put frequent little milestones in my tactical plan so I can feel like I am moving forward.

This is especially important if your dream is something that will take some time – a few years, perhaps. It's very easy to get frustrated when you just have one goal – the end goal. Give yourself those little victories along the way.

Building Blocks for an Effective Road Map - Where Do I Want to Go?

I used this illustration before, but it works here very well. When I want to know how to get from my house in Hanover, PA to look at a potential property in Fairborn, OH, I need to know three things - and these may seem trivial but there is a point. First, I need to know where I am. Second, I need to know where I am going. Third, I need to figure out how to get from where I am to where I am going. If I ask my sister in Lancaster, CA how she would get to Fairborn, OH it would be pretty useless. She is starting from a different point than me. Even if I asked my best friend, who lives about 15 miles from me, it would not be very helpful.

In Chapter I, we wrote down our *Precious Burning Desire* - we even turned that desire into a SMART Goal. If you recall, the SMART Goal consisted of:

- Specific
- Measurable
- Ambitious
- Realistic
- Timely

This goes a long way to helping you realize your dream, when we take it from just a dream to a goal. But, this also begs the question, how do we reach that goal? This is where we are going. In this chapter, we will talk about building an effective plan to get there. Go back and re-evaluate your SMART Goal. Now that you have gotten the firsthand knowledge (from the last chapter) to accomplish your goals, has this caused you to modify your goal (not your desire, but the physical manifestation of that desire)?

Building Blocks for an Effective Road Map - Where Am I Now?

But, in order for the plan to be useful to *YOU*, it must be designed to start where *YOU* are located. In one of our case studies I am talking about trying to lose weight while I am writing this book. I need to lose about 100 pounds. If I looked at a plan for someone that only needed to lose 10 pounds, that would not be very useful. I'm not 10 pounds overweight, I am 100 pounds overweight. I need a plan that starts with someone that is 100 pounds overweight.

Building Blocks for an Effective Road Map - How Do I Get There From Here?

Now, you are ready to build your plan. This will be your roadmap to take you from where you are today to realizing your *Precious Burning Desire*. And, we are not going to build just one plan, but two.

First, we will build the strategic plan or, actually, two strategic plans. If you are trying to get fit, these are your fitness plans. If you are an entrepreneur, these are the same as your business plans. The strategic plan is, basically, your big picture. It gives you a mountain top view of getting from where you are today to where you want to be.

The first type of strategic plan is the Strategic Growth Plan. This is the plan that tells you exactly how to get from where you are to where you want to be. This plan is your road map to get you from where you are today to where you want to be. This plan can cover anywhere from a month or so to a couple of years.

The second type of strategic plan is the Static Strategic Plan. Your Static Strategic Plan usually spans years. It can be anywhere from 2-3 years to 5-20 years. We will talk about two types of strategic plans – growth and static.

Strategic Growth Plan

Your strategic plan is your "big picture" plan. It tells you what you are doing over the long haul to get to your goal. As I said above, the Strategic Growth Plan is great for getting you from where you are now to realizing your *Precious Burning Desire.* The best way to build this plan is with the help of a coach and mentor. However, I want to put together two quick examples (fitness and business) to give you an idea of how to build your Strategic Growth Plan.

Strategic Growth Plan for Fitness

If you have ever tried to get in shape, you probably know you shouldn't just jump into the gym at full tilt. And, you probably shouldn't cut out everything you are not supposed to eat only to be replaced by perfect food. Let's go over a few things that might go into a Fitness Growth Strategic Plan:

1. Coach/Mentor. One of the first things you probably want to do is interview and select a coach and/or fitness mentor who meet all the criteria we talked about in the last chapter.

2. Physical. Take a physical. You need to know your body.

I was a professional athlete in my 20s. Now, I am just about 60-years-old. Trust me, I don't have the same body. Things I could get away with 30 and 40 years ago, well, not so much now. As you put your plan together, let your doctor have some input.

3. Gym. So, where are you going to work out? Is there a gym near your house? Does your fitness coach/mentor have a favorite place to meet with you?

4. Aerobics. You need to determine the heart rate you want to use when you are doing your aerobic exercise. Then, you need to make a gradual plan to increase the intensity of your training as you get in better shape. Of course, you will not be able to do as much at first as you will be able to do later in your program.

5. Weight Training. First, even if your goal is "just to lose weight," you still need to lift weights. And, if you have never done this before, it behooves you to go slow, learn right the first time, and build a good base.

6. Nutrition. By now, if you followed the advice in *Chapter IV: Firsthand Knowledge*, took the classes and hired a coach/mentor, you have probably learned what you need to know about macro-nutrients, micro-nutrients, supplements, vitamins, and minerals. But, theory is different than practice. Take it slow. Follow your coach/mentor's advice. If you are doing this on your own, maybe take a month to figure out what combinations work best for your body.

As you can see, even though there is not a lot to prep you still would be served well to create a Strategic Growth Plan for your fitness goals. Now, let's see how this plans plays out in the business world.

Strategic Growth Plan for Business

This is a much more complicated situation than the fitness plan. There are a lot of things demanding your full attention when you want to start a business. To get a feel for all that needs to be considered when starting your business, let's build an online training company together. Maybe, we want to build a company that teaches how to make origami birds – those little paper birds they make at Japanese restaurants.

1. Market Analysis. The very first step is to see if there is a market for online origami training. A good place to start looking is www.ClickBank.com. You can use this website to see what is selling on the net.

2. Company Registration. What type of company will you have? You can do a corporation, an LLC, or an LP, for example.

3. Branding. Once you figure out what people need and are willing to pay for, your next step is to work out your branding. This includes things like figuring out your color scheme and fonts, looking at your web presence and design, maybe your Facebook group and other social media presence.

4. Marketing and Sales Funnel. You need to decide how you are going to reach your target market. Are you going to use Google AdWords? Will you place ads on Facebook? Do you know who your target market is and where they hang out online? Will you build your own sales funnels or will you use a website like

www.ClickFunnels.com? What about autoresponder email services?

5. Joint Venture (JV) Partners. You can use JV partners to sale your training. Or, especially at the start of our company, you can sale the products of your JV partners.

6. Training Development. You need to build your training. Will you use live video or something like PowerPoint? Will you host the training on something like www.Memberium.com or just put them on YouTube or www.Vimeo.com?

7. Will you have levels of training? Maybe teach how to make some easy birds in your first course. Then, for those who are good at origami, offer a more advanced course.

8. Merchant Account. How will you accept payments? There are several great merchant account firms on the internet.

9. Associated Sales. Will you offer anything else for sale? Maybe you can offer origami paper. Or, if it really takes off, you could do an annual conference or monthly seminars.

No matter what our Precious Burning Desire, you NEED a Strategic Growth Plan. This plan is going to tell you:

- Where you are now
- Where you want to go
- Why you want to go there
- How you are going to get there

- Who is going to help you get there
- What strengths and weaknesses do you have
- When do you plan on arriving at your goal

As you can see, these are items you need to deal with at the start of your company. But probably don't want them reflected in your Static Strategic Plan. You need them in your Strategic Growth Plan.

Building Blocks for an Effective Road Map - How Do I Stay There?

If your Strategic Growth Plan gets you to your destination, what do you do when you get there? It's not enough to lose the weight and get the body you want You need to figure out how to keep that body. It's not enough to grow a business to the level of your dreams. How do you keep it running like a well-oiled machine? This is the job of your Static Strategic Plan.

Static Strategic Plan

What I mean by static, is a plan that does not change much. You have an established business or fitness plan where things are working pretty well. Your Static Strategic Plan for fitness might be called your maintenance plan. You don't really want to make any massive changes. You have already gone through the growth phase to get to this point.

What I want to do here is give you an outline and explanation of the various parts of a Static Strategic Plan. I'll talk very briefly about a maintenance plan for fitness then I want to spend a bit more time talking about a long term business plan.

Static Strategic Plan for Fitness

The good news here is, you can probably cut down on your exercising and increase what you eat every day. The bad news is, unless you have a plan you follow religiously, you will probably back slide to where you started (or, worse). At least, I know I did.

By the time you get to the maintenance phase, you should know a lot about nutrition and exercise. You should also know a lot about how your body reacts to what you eat and what you do. This will help you build your maintenance plan. Here are some things to consider when building your plan (however, it is best to consult with your coach/mentor):

Exercise. You probably have gotten used to doing aerobics every morning for six days a week and lifting weights every afternoon three or six times a week. During maintenance, you can probably cut this in half. What I have done for this phase is work out six mornings a week, alternating between aerobics and weight training.

Nutrition. Basically, here I am talking about the calories you take in every day. You need to calculate your new calorie burn from your reduced exercise, and what you are burning throughout the day. Then, that tells you what calories you should eat every day. Keep in mind, you probably want to keep your proteins where they were during your Strategic Growth Plan. So, the real good news is, you are probably going to increase your calories through carbs. But, make sure they are good carbs!

Iteration. As you go through your Maintenance Plan, you will find things do not always go exactly like you expected. You will probably have to tweak the plan. If your original growth plan was to lose weight, you need to monitor that and make sure you are not losing too much weight or, perhaps, gaining a little weight. You can play with exercise and nutrition to fix this.

Static Strategic Plan for Business

When most people talk about a business plan they are talking about the Static Strategic Plan. What I am going to do on the next couple of pages is just lay out some of the more important sections you should include in your plan. But, this is just a starting point. What you really need to do is get with your coach/mentor and map out the business plan that is structured specifically for your company.

Mission Statement. This is a restatement of the goal you set back in Chapter I. What you want to do is take the goal from your Precious Burning Desire and massage it into a single sentence. My goal for my real estate business was to provide affordable houses to middle class families. Here was my mission statement: "The mission of ***Woodburn Management, LP*** is to purchase properties through various acquisition strategies and provide them at less than fair market value to middle class families."

Executive Summary. Some people look at the executive summary as an outline of your entire strategic plan. I like to use it as an expansion and explanation of my Mission Statement.

SWOT (Strengths, Weaknesses, Opportunities and Threats). This is a great place to evaluate where you are as our business reaches steady state. This section is to address YOUR strengths and weaknesses. It is also a great place to list the opportunities and threats you will face as you work to reach your goals.

Legal/Business Structure. This one really is particular to a business plan and doesn't lend itself to something like a fitness plan (unless, of course, you plan to market your awesome gains). Here you will list the type of business structure you have and, perhaps, why you chose the particular legal structure you did. Are you a Limited Partner (LP), a Limited Liability Company (LLC), a C-Corporations, or an S-Corporation? You could even be a not-for-profit company like a 501(c)(3). Where the Legal Description gives a legal idea of your company the Business Structure gives a physical description.

Product Description. What product or services do you provide? Again, this section does not lend itself to something like fitness.

Intellectual Property Description. This covers things like books, articles, logos, and any web presence.

Location. This is simply your address or addresses. At the time we wrote our business plan, we had offices in four states (PA, OH, MD, AZ). We included all of the address and noted which one was the headquarters.

Management and Personnel. This section is rather long and the title is fairly self-explanatory. You want to record who manages the various parts of your company and how they will manage your company.

Records. Where do you keep your financial records,

legal records, and general book keeping records? When you first start, they are probably at your home (especially if you have a home-based business). Eventually, you will probably keep your financial records at your accountant's office. You will keep your legal records at your attorney's office. And, you will keep your book keeping records with your book keeper.

Insurance. Another self-explanatory section. You need insurance. But, what type? My best advice is to ask your attorney or someone who handles business insurance in your particular field.

Litigation. Really, what you are saying in this section is that no one who has an interest in your company is under a current litigation when you start your business.

Risks. This is very similar to the threat part of SWOT section. However, I use Risks to talk about internal problems that may occur. I use Threats to talk about external factors that may influence the success of my company.

Branding. Who are you? This is the question that branding answers. Branding is a lot more than just a logo and a flashy website. It's beyond the scope of this book but, if you are serious about having an impact on the world through your business, you need to brand. You need to learn how to build your branding bible. There are a lot of websites that can help you with this. They can help with logos, color schemes, fonts - everything you need to let people know you are there and that you have a unique solution to their problem.

Marketing. There is so much you can do here. You

need to address markcts, competition, marketing strategies, industry and market trends. As a matter of fact, as an entrepreneur, you should spend about 90% of your time on this one thing – marketing.

Sales. Marketing brings people into our sales funnel. But, once they are there, what do you do to keep them and to turn them from prospects to customers.

Financials. Your financials are your scorecard. This is how you tell you are successful or, um, not so successful. If a business is not tracking their cashflow, then it isn't really a business but, rather, it's a hobby. If you are not good with numbers, I would suggest you get a bookkeeper. I'll be honest with you, tracking financials are very depressing when you first start and not making any money. But, when success starts to build, it's nice to know where you stand. This will also give you indications on how you can scale your business to make whatever income you need or desire.

Dealing with the Day-to-Day – Your Tactical Plan

Once you have the strategic plan, then you are ready to build your tactical plan. Basically, the tactical plan is your day-to-day resource on what you need to do to hit each and every milestone in your strategic plan.

Tactical Plan for Fitness

Once you determined (in your strategic plan) what you want to weigh, what percent body fat did you want, and how long did you plan to get there – then you are ready for your tactical plan. This would cover things like:

- What foods do you eat every meal

- What macronutrients (protein powder, etc) do you eat every day
- What micronutrients (supplements, vitamins) do you take every day
- How much water do you drink every day
- What type of aerobic exercise do you do, when and how frequently
- What type of anaerobic exercise, when and how long

Tactical Plan for Business

For my real estate companies, the tactical plan had 3 parts:

1. ***Property Acquisition***. This section of my tactical plan was dozens of pages long. It covered everything. It covered how to acquire properties (tax deed auctions, foreclosures, wholesalers, short sales). It covered how many phone calls had to be made each day for each type of acquisition strategy to ensure our quotas were met. It covered how many auctions our teams had to cover each week. It covered how to get funds for the different acquisition strategies (banks, hard money lenders, investors, debt partners). It covered how to price the properties (cost of money, cost of acquisition, cost of purchase, cost of rehab, cost of holding, cost of taxes/insurance, cost of selling).

2. ***Rehab of properties***. This covered what teams to use for which properties. It talked about the different rehab strategy based on whether we were planning to rent or sale the property.

3. ***Disposition of properties***. This section of the tactical

plan talked about the different exit strategies we could use for each property. It covered fix and flip, rentals, lease with an option to buy, land contract, and sell to another investor (wholesale).

Hopefully this gives you a good framework on how to construct your strategic and tactical plans. If you want to be successful, you NEED to have both of these plans set up and you NEED to follow them. If, as you follow your plans, you are not reaching your goals, don't drop the plans. Figure out what is wrong. Write it out. Then follow the improved plan.

Case Study I: Evangelist

Since this is the most mature of the case studies, I wanted to talk a bit about evolving plans and focus on the *Precious Burning Desire*. When I first learned to witness (tell others about Jesus and what He can do for them) I was content to just go out on my own (with Cathy, of course) and talk to people one-on-one.

Eventually, this wasn't enough. I hooked up with a local outreach pastor (never knew those existed before) and he showed me how to set up booths/tents at local fairs, carnivals and craft shows where a group of us could talk to thousands of people in a week.

Eventually, we got to talking about how many local pastors are not able to show their people how to share their faith. This led to the creation of our first evangelism ministry and us doing evangelism conferences for pastors in third world countries.

We now have four different trainings we offer to

churches and Christian groups through the ***Lura B Walker Foundation*** with the accompanying plans and processes:

1. ***Marketplace Evangelism***. We work with local churches to set up evangelism tents in fairs, carnivals, craft shows, and various venues where people hang out.

2. ***Short Term Mission Trips***. Before a church group goes on a mission trip, we prepare them to share their faith in an easy and non-threatening way.

3. ***Everyday Evangelism***. We have a home study course for the outreach pastor of a church. This is also reflected in a live 3-day event to help jump start any church's evangelism program. We train church leadership to re-focus their church to be more evangelistically oriented. We show the staff how to witness and how to set up permanent training programs to train their church members.

4. ***Revive Us Again***. This is the program that travels to third world countries. We have a three day seminar where we train local pastors in the Great Commission. We do this using both a classroom environment and actual field work.

Case Study 2: Real Estate Investing

One of the biggest advantages of the *Rich Dad Education* classes was the plan of action given out at the end of each class. I was well equipped to hit the ground running when I would return from a three day course. Our investing was in two phases:

Residential Phase: In this phase we would buy houses

at tax deed auctions in Ohio. It went something like this:

1. Find areas where we would like to invest
2. Pick houses going up for auction that would be worth owning
3. Go to the auction and NOT bid too much
4. Renovate the house
5. Refinance the houses so that we were using none of our own money.
6. Put the house up for sale (through Land Contract)
7. Collect the monthly passive income.

Commercial Phase: We found that, even though we were making money with residential investing, the money was not coming fast enough to really help our ministry. We made the decision to take our residential experience (along with a couple of more classes from *Rich Dad Education*) and apply them to commercial investing. The plan was fairly similar:

1. Determine area to invest.
2. Evaluate apartment complexes (five per week)
3. Make offers on potential good deals (about 1 out of every 100)
4. Find equity partners (people with money) to invest with us
5. Find banks that would be our debt partners
6. Work through our Due Diligence to make sure the deal was good
7. Find a property manager to manage the property
8. Collect the monthly passive income.

Case Study 3: Getting in Shape

Once I decided I would get in shape, I needed a viable

plan for getting in shape. My plan was fairly basic:

1. Map out the calories for the duration: 2,000 calories (50% protein, 25% each carbs and fat).
2. When we first get out of bed in the morning we will do 30 minutes of stationary bike riding in our basement gym.
3. After dinner, one hour of weight training back down in the basement gym.
4. Rest every seventh day.

I know this is a LOT of activity. Fortunately, our investing has given me some freedom to spend this much time to get in shape. This is a great blessing that I need to take advantage of. Also, this allowed me to be able to slip if life got too busy. I could afford to skip one of my daily activities – usually the afternoon hike, if necessary.

EXERCISES

1. Write out your goal

2. Build the parts of your Strategic Growth Plan.

3. Build your tactical plan (be as detailed as possible)

Doin' the Dream

시작이 반이다

The above writing is a Korean proverb. It says, "Well begun is half done." And, if you have followed the steps so far, you are well past half done. You walked through *Going for the Gold* where you fixed the inner game of success. Once you were prepared on the inside, you *Organized for Success* by putting together your positive affirmations, learned what you needed to win, and built a plan on that knowledge.

Victory is almost guaranteed. It's now just a matter of going through the motions. Its time to *Do the Dream.*

VI. Concrete Action

Even so faith, if it hath not works, is dead, being alone.
(James 2:14)

Usually, if someone is to fail, it will be at this point. It's one thing to have a dream, build up your faith and develop a plan. But, boy, when you actually have to pull the trigger and turn theory into practical application – now it's real! I have talked to several very successful business people. Every single one of them told me they think this is *THE* most important step to success.

Bob's Story

Back in *Chapter II: Exercise Your Faith Not Your Fear,* I talked about the first investment house we bought. Recall, it was at a tax deed auction. You may recall, I just mentioned in passing that it was an emotional roller coaster. Let me talk about that here.

I had taken a couple of real estate classes from James Smith (prior to joining *Rich Dad Education*) and I was thinking about it being time to "pull the trigger" on buying my first property. Of course, I was scared to death. I was going to spend a boat load of money on a process I had never vetted personally. I was scheduled to take a few more classes, so I thought to do a survey.

Every time I would show up at a class, I would engage as many other students as I could. I would ask two questions. First, I asked them how many classes they had taken (I think there were about 10 different classes you could take). Second, I asked them how many investment houses they had bought since they started the classes.

It was very eye-opening. The number of classes was all over the place. Everywhere from "This is my first class." To "I've taken all the classes and now I am taking some over again – they were SO great." But, wouldn't you know, every single one of them said, "Nope, I haven't bought an investment house, yet." Not a single person had pulled the trigger! What was going on?

No, I didn't interview every single student so there could have been a few who did a deal. But, boy, it sure set a trend. After the third course with interviews, I got home from Scottsdale, AZ and I told Cathy, "I am not going to another course until we own a property!"

Later, I would interview several successful men and women to get their opinions on the ***7 PERFECT Steps to Success***. One of the questions I asked each of them was, "Which one of the steps to you find to be the hardest." To a person, each of them said, "Concrete Action, Step #6." They all told me the scariest thing was taking that first, real, step. And, that is what I found out in my casual survey of real estate investment students. None of them had what it took to pull the trigger.

Because I had already trained myself and used the ***7 PERFECT Steps to Success***, I was able to buy that first house at the tax deed auction and move to making over a million dollars in real estate.

ELISHA

Elijah had lived a full, productive life for the Lord. It was time for him to pick a successor and then be taken to heaven. Elisha was determined to be that successor. As Elijah went to cross the Jordon River, Elisha followed close behind. When they came to the river, Elijah took off his coat and hit the waters and the waters parted. The two men walked across on dry land.

Finally, Elijah said, "Ask what I shall do for thee, before I be taken away from thee."

And Elisha said, "I pray thee, let a double portion of thy spirit be upon me."

Elijah told Elisha, "Thou hast asked a hard thing: nevertheless, if thou see me when I am taken from thee, it shall be so unto thee; but if not, it shall not be so."

Elisha was there to watch as the chariots of fire came down from heaven and took Elijah and he went up in a whirlwind as his coat fell to the ground. Elisha fulfilled his part of the bargain, he saw Elijah taken to heaven. He had every right to expect God to uphold His part of the deal. But, he didn't just sit around and wait for God to act. No, instead Elisha took action himself. And, he did it right away.

Elisha picked up Elijah's coat and walked to the Jordan

River. When he got there, he hit the waters with the coat and he said, "Where is the Lord God of Elijah?" And the waters parted. Elisha took concrete action and things happened!

Elisha went on to perform twice as many miracles as Elijah.

WHY IS IT HARD TO START?

When I first started writing this book, I wanted to make sure my steps to success resonated with other successful men and women. I started interviewing every successful person I could find. I talked to doctors and lawyers. I talked to business owners and pastors and priests. Every time I interviewed someone, I'd ask them for people they knew who I should interview.

What I would do in these interviews is show them a list of the ***7 PERFECT Steps to Success*** (not the whole book, just an outline of the steps, themselves). I would go over each step and what I thought they meant. Then, after I went over this as a background, I would start the interview. One of the questions I always asked was, "What do you think is the hardest of the 7 steps?"

I was shocked. Every single person said the same thing. I mean, 100% of them, not a single outlier. All of them said that starting, taking the first step, was the hardest thing they ever did on their road to success.

Even if you have followed the first five of the ***7 PERFECT Steps to Success***, when you get to this step you are going from a theory to real life. Let's do a quick review of how we got to this point.

Going for the Gold

This first section of the book was all about working on winning the inner game. Winning the inner game is critical to success.

Precious Burning Desire. The first thing we did was work on turning your dream into a *Precious Burning Desire.* We looked at aligning your conscious and sub-conscious with your dream. Then, we turned your dream from a *Precious Burning Desire* into an actionable goal.

Exercise Your Faith Not Your Fear. In this chapter, we worked on building your faith. We saw that God and the universe were not out to get you. We looked at how you can move toward your goals with faith in a process while you built faith in yourself. We also spent some time looking at ways to deal with different types of fear.

Organizing for Success

Once the inner game is tackled, the next thing you need to do is set yourself up for success in the outer game. That was the purpose of the second section of the book.

Repeat After Me. Here we saw just how powerful positive affirmations can be in moving from the inner game to the real world.

Firsthand Knowledge. Too many people try to just jump into reaching their dream without really learning what they need to guarantee success. As a matter of fact, some business coaches say things like, "All you have to do is ready, fire, aim." In other words, figure it out as you go. Not a good idea. In this chapter, we talked about the best ways to get the knowledge you need to be successful.

Effective Planning. Once you have your dream in place, you've learned to have faith in what you are doing, you've put together your positive affirmations, and learned the skill sets to turn your dream into a reality – you are ready to build your plans. That is the point of this chapter. We talked about building a Strategic Growth Plan, a Static Strategic Plan, and a Tactical Plan.

So, the bottom line, you have done everything possible to guarantee your success. If you have taken these five steps to heart, you are more prepare than anyone else on the planet. You WILL be successful! However, you still might find yourself hesitating to pull the trigger. Let's spend a bit of time talking about that and see if we can't help you take this most important step.

WHY DON'T WE JUST START?

Before we jump into actually taking *Concrete Action*, I want to spend some time looking at why this is such a hard step for everyone. Here are some of the reasons people have a hard time taking *Concrete Action*:

Inertia. Even though you really want to see your *Precious Burning Desire* come to life, sometimes simple inertia stops us from moving forward. Life just gets in the way. If you have a big dream (and, if you have made it this far through the book, you probably do), then it is going to take a lot of time and energy to bring it to life. But, you probably also have most of your day filled with important things that MUST get done for you to survive. You have to find a way past the inertia of your day-to-day life and find new room for your dream.

Fear of Failure. This is big. A lot of people, when they start thinking about actually going for the dream of a lifetime stop because they are afraid they will fail. They think there is just no way the *Precious Burning Desire* can actually work. I mean, after all, it hasn't worked, yet. What makes me think I can make it work now.

Fear of Inadequacy. This is similar to the last reason. You feel like your dream is possible but not with you in the driver's seat. You think that, maybe, someone can do it. Just not you.

A Step Into Reality. I think all of these reasons boil down to this one fact. You are getting ready to take a dream you have held in your heart (so, it is really special to you) and you are afraid it might not be real. When you take that first step, it is a very serious commitment. You are saying to the world, "This isn't just a dream this is something that will really happen," Psychologically, this is night and day. One moment it is just a dream, a fantasy, the next you are seriously pursuing it. This is a big deal. Don't minimize the feelings but, instead, deal with them and move forward. You really can do this. You, personally, CAN reach your most *Precious Burning Desire*. Take the step! You will be so happy you did.

Four Steps to Starting Your Dream

If you are able to pull the trigger and take *Concrete Action*, awesome! However, if you are still feeling a little jittery, then let's walk through four steps that can help you get over the hump.

Think About Your *Precious Burning Desire*

The first thing I want you to do is a little craft project. Here is what you will need:

- Poster Board
- Markers
- Pictures reminding you of your *Precious Burning Desire*
- Glue or glue stick

Now, what I want you to do is make a vision board for your *Precious Burning Desire.* And, yes, this is the vision board we talked about in *Chapter IV: Repeat After Me* – I just know some people reading this book have not done that, yet. I want you to build something that will hit all learning styles: auditory, tactile, and visual. And I want you to spend extra time on your particular learning style. Once the board is built, I need you to find a place to hang it where you will see it first thing in the morning and just before you go to bed at night.

For a week, I want you to stand in front of the board at least twice each day. When you are standing in front of it, I want you to scan everything you made on the board and feel (yes, *feel*) what it will be like when you reach your dream. Revel in the feeling and make it real.

The second thing I want you to do is get several 3x5 cards. Write out the positive affirmations you made back in *Chapter III: Repeat After Me.* I want you to keep a set by your bed or by your bathroom sink. I want you to keep a set at your work location and I want you to keep a set on your person at all times (OK, maybe not in the shower, but all other times).

When you are standing in front of your dream board, after you have spent a few minutes reveling in the feeling of success, I want you to read your affirmations with that feeling in your heart.

Understand, No Movement Means No Dream

If the above is not enough to get you moving. Another thing you can do, though it is a bit negative, is to think and feel what it will be like for you and the world, if you never achieve your dream. Realize, if you don't act your dream will never come to pass. Or, worse (for me), someone else will feel led to take up your dream and you get to watch them in the place designed specifically for you.

I would only use this step sparingly and in emergencies.

Follow Your Tactical Plan

Once you are set on exactly what your *Precious Burning Desire* is, it's time to act. When you are ready to act, remember, you don't have to do it all at once. All you have to do is the first step.

What I would suggest is taking out your tactical plan and mapping out the first step.

If your goal is to get in shape, maybe your first step is looking on the internet for a fitness coach in your area. Maybe lay out the websites you found and any email or phone numbers on the site. And that would be it for the day. You started reaching your *Precious Burning Desire.* Wasn't that simple? The next day you can deal with deciding if you will call them or email them and what you will say.

If your goal is to start your own business, maybe the first step can be calling the IRS to get an EIN (Employee Identification Number) for your company. Make it real. The EIN is, for a company, what the social security number is for a person. Maybe, the next day, you can look at how to register your new company with the state you are living in or the state you want to register the company in.

The idea is, your first step doesn't have to be something big. It just has to be something you DO.

Celebrate

This may sound silly to you but it really is very important. After you take the first physical action to make your dream a reality, I want you to celebrate. I have started several *Precious Burning Desires* and, unfortunately, I have let some slip away. I know how significant it is to actually start.

So, yes, celebrate. Whatever it is you do to make a big deal out of an event, do it (unless, of course, what you usually do is eat a big meal and you are trying to get in shape – maybe, then, buy yourself something). But, the point is, I want you to mark this first step as the first step of your big dream. It really is a very big deal!

As a matter of fact, one of the things I would like you to do for me is, go to the Life Changers 180 Facebook group (www.Facebook.com/LifeChangers180), join and share…

- Your *Precious Burning Desire*
- What you did for your very first step
- What you did to celebrate

The Two Excuses You Will Run Into

There are two extremes you can face when you are getting ready to start any project. You can be the "I know everything I'm just going to start" guy or the "I still need more data before I do anything" guy.

Know it All. If this has been you in the past and you have experienced your fair share of failures, you might feel apprehensive about taking on something as close to your heart as this dream. If you have followed everything we have talked about so far in the ***7 PERFECT Steps to Success*** then, this time, you really do know enough to start.

Don't Know Enough. Are you the type who is guilty of analysis paralysis? You keep studying and studying but never do anything? I spent most of my adult life as a scientist and engineer. I can really relate to this personality. You never want to pull the trigger because you think there is always something else out there you need to learn. There's one last piece of data that will make everything fall perfectly into place. Just like the *Know It All* group, if you have followed everything we have talked about so far in the ***7 PERFECT Steps to Success*** then, this time, you really do know enough to start.

Let the Party Begin!

Now, there should be nothing left to stop you from taking that first, all important, step.

Case Study 1: Evangelist

Back in *Chapter IV: Firsthand Knowledge*, I talked about how I went out for six months to try to do whatever it was an evangelist was supposed to do. I guess I fell into the "know it all" category this time. If I didn't have such *Tenacious Persistence* (the topic of the next chapter), I would have quit. I was so not prepared to take *Concrete Action*. I eventually learned how to effectively share Jesus with others. But, I sure could have saved a boat load of pain and misery on my part if I had made sure I had the inner game set and organized for success by learning what I really needed to do and built a plan to effectively do it.

Case Study 2: Real Estate Investing

At the beginning of this chapter, I talked about going to all the real estate investment classes and finding person after person who never pulled the trigger. I met so many people who fit the "don't know enough" category. I actually spent most of my adult life as a physicist and astronautical engineer. Because of this, I can recognize this personality trait a mile away. But, fortunately, I was able to break this mold and buy my first house.

Case Study 3: Getting in Shape

By the time I made the decision to really get in shape, I had formulated the ***7 PERFECT Steps to Success***. I was able to put what I have in this book to the test. It was real easy to pull the trigger this time. It felt right. I had a very serious *Precious Burning Desire* – I spent a few days in the hospital with heart problems about a year ago. The doctor, with a stern look and a wagging finger, told me I HAD to get in shape. And, I already had faith in myself – I spent about 12 years as a professional fighter and another 15 years as a professional dancer. I knew I could do it. I put together some affirmations and built a vision board, I even got myself a coach/mentor – the head of the ***Life Changers 180's*** fitness division.

Exercises

1. Create your dream board.
2. Write out what your first step will be.
3. Do it!
4. Write out how you will celebrate.
5. Do it!

VII. Tenacious Persistence

For a just man falleth seven times, and riseth up again: but the wicked shall fall into mischief. (Proverbs 24:16)

Winston Churchill once said, "Never give in, never give in, never; never; never; never - in nothing, great or small, large or petty - never give in except to convictions of honor and good sense." Imagine how the world would be if babies stopped trying to walk after their first, second, or (even) hundredth time trying. Imagine how the world would be if small children gave up trying to form sentences to communicate with others. Imagine how the world would be if you never pursued your *Precious Burning Desire.* Never give in, never give up.

Bob's Story

I sat across the table from Robin Srempek in the Morning Room of my house. It was July 5, 2015. I had conceived of the idea for this book months earlier. But, I wanted more. I knew this book could help thousands of people around the world. But, I also knew, just reading a book doesn't always get people into action. I had gone to a few motivational seminars and seen what they could do. Some were really great. Some, well, not really great.

I wanted to bounce my ideas off Robin and get her input. I thought to have a series of live trainings that were after the tradition of motivational seminars but with a significant difference – where motivational speakers stopped with fixing the inside of a person, I wanted to continue until I could actually see my students be successful.

Robin was the perfect choice for a partner. She had tried the ***7 PERFECT Steps to Success*** in her own life to: (1) lose 100 pounds in 18 months and keep it off for several years, (2) increase her credit score 333 points in a year, and (3) completely change her career from middle school music teacher to IT expert. She had a master's degree in music education. She was a National Board Certified Teacher in adolescence and young adults for music. She was an active member in the local Toast Masters. Basically, she knew how to teach a complicated subject (music) to a group of people who were not the most motivated in the world (middle school students). She, also, had an intimate and personal knowledge of the subject I wanted to share with the world – ***7 PERFECT Steps to Success***.

She not only jumped on board right away – she loved the idea – but, she volunteered to become a partner in the new company and take on the role of CEO. Homerun!

The first several months were awesome. We developed curriculum based on the content of the book you are holding in your hands. We put the word out that we were the new kids in town. It was just a matter of sitting back and watching the throngs of people show up at our live events.

By December of 2015, it was obvious this business was different from all the others I had successfully built. I didn't realize it at the time but, I never really had to worry about marketing in my other companies. My martial arts studios were all on military bases or next to them. Word of mouth worked like a charm. My aerospace software consulting company had a built-in customer base before I opened the doors. My real estate companies found derelict buildings that we rehabbed and left up to our real estate agent to market and sale.

So, Robin and I found a big hole in our business model that hit us by surprise. The perfect image of our defeat was a conference room we had rented in a hotel near Washington, DC. The room was set up for 100 people. We had five staff show up and a grand total of four students show up. IF we were going to be successful, we HAD to figure out how to market ourselves.

Our goal was to help about 100 to 200 people a month. Four is a loooong way from that goal. What we had going for us:

- We had a Precious Burning Desire in our hearts to help people be successful.
- We had faith in our process. Everything (except the marketing) worked great.
- We knew our subject intimately. I spent my entire adult life applying the ***7 PERFECT Steps to Success***. Robin had been using them over the past few years.
- We had a great plan for success – with one major hole.

But the rest was there.

Fortunately, we were able to map out all of this and it really helped our faith. Now, it was time to get down to business and figure out how to market to the world. We knew our marketing had to be online in order to reach the numbers of people we wanted to help. It took us an entire year, several thousand dollars, and three different online marketing companies before we found a match to us with a group that could help us launch the volume we needed.

There were times during that year when the entire company basically came to a standstill. Frustration and despair could have shut us down. We just knew the first marketing firm we hired to teach us would be the golden ticket we needed. We were wrong. Then, we just knew the second marketing firm we hired to teach us would be the golden ticket we needed. We were wrong, again. Boy, that can knock the wind out of your sails. Then, we just knew the third marketing firm we hired to teach us would be the golden ticket we needed. And, drum roll, they were!!!

We had hit a point of despair but we stuck it out and it paid off. Now, you are holding this book in your hands and there are over a hundred people every month learning to be successful using the tools presented in these pages.

JACOB

Tenacious persistence. That's the title of this chapter. If there's an award for the most tenaciously persistent person in ALL of history, it must go to Jacob. Let me tell you what happened.

Jacob had travelled back to his mom’s home town to

find a bride. As a matter of fact, he was headed to his grandfather's house. As he drew near the town, he stopped at a watering hole where he met the woman of his dreams – Rachel.

Jacob's Uncle Laban had two daughters – Leah (the oldest) and Rachel. Jacob took a job with his uncle and grew to love Rachel. As a laborer in his uncle's sheep business, he had no means. But, he loved Rachel so much, he made a deal with his uncle. Jacob would work for 7 years (7 YEARS) in order to marry his love. Okay, how many men would do that?

After the 7 years were over, there was a wedding. Now, in that time in history, a wedding was a really long party with LOTS of drinking. They drank for about a week. At the end of the week, the groom would go into the bride and consummate the marriage.

Ole Uncle Laban banked on Jacob being so drunk he wouldn't know who he spent the night with. When Jacob woke up the next morning he was in bed next to Leah. He just married the wrong sister! Laban's excuse was the younger daughter should not get married before the older daughter. But, wrong is wrong.

Jacob was able to marry Rachel right away. But, he had to promise to work another 7 years for the privilege.

Wow! Can you imagine having to work for 7 YEARS to marry the girl of your dreams only to be tricked and having to work ANOTHER 7 years? He showed incredible persistence here – a VERY positive character trait. Now, he didn't start off as a paragon of virtue – he stole his brother, Esau's, birthright. But, this persistence would serve him very well in the future.

The Success Curve

In *Chapter IV: Firsthand Knowledge*, we quoted Sun Tzu:

> *"To be victorious in battle, know your enemy, know yourself, and know your environment." Sun Tzu*

If you recall, we interpreted these three as know your goal, know yourself, and know your environment. We spent a bit of time on the first two but just brushed over the last one (know your environment). Now, I'd like to spend some time on it. But first, let's do a fast review of the first two.

Know Your Goal. If you have been working your *Precious Burning Desire* while reading this book and did the exercises in Chapters I and IV, then you have this nailed. Then, in Chapter V, we brought this home by building an effective plan based on your goals.

Know Yourself. Again, we spent a bit of time on this in Chapter I. In particular, we made sure your comforts and cringes lined up with your *Precious Burning Desire*.

Know Your Environment. One of the things I learned in my 20 years in the military is the first casualty of war is the war plan. So, you might say, "Then why have a plan to begin with?" Well, turns out, no plan is a guarantee of failure. At least, with a plan, you know when things aren't going right and you can apply some stick and rudder (a Navy term for guidance) to your problem. What I want to focus on now is the greatest cause of killing the plan – ***The Success Curve***. The Success Curve is the environment you will live in when you move to accomplish your dream, your *Precious Burning Desire.*

I first heard of this curve in the entrepreneurial world. But, it really applies to any pursuit of success you have. As you can see, the curve has three legs, an up, a down, and

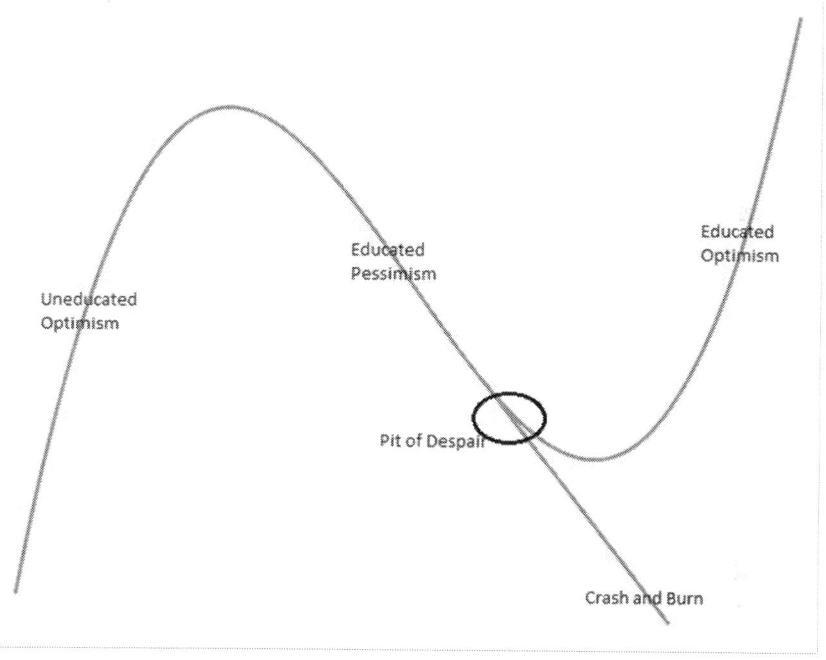

another up (with that little leg at the bottom). Let's look at what it means to you.

Uneducated Optimism. This is where you first had the idea to start a business, loss weight or pursue some goal close to your heart.

Maybe the business was your own creation. Maybe it was a multi-level marketing opportunity you just couldn't pass up. Maybe you went to a seminar and someone showed you how this particular business was going to make you rich.

Maybe you just wanted to fit into your new dress for the wedding of a friend. Maybe your doctor told you that you were pre-diabetic and you had to lose weight. Maybe you decided to run your first marathon.

You stepped out in faith and just knew the world was waiting for what you had to offer. Everything was sunshine and unicorns. It was all new and you couldn't wait, every day, to jump in with both feet to see what would happen. You were sure victory was right around the corner.

The feeling you have during this phase of your adventure is one of the greatest feelings in the world. But hold on, in a few minutes we will see that there is even a better feeling. But first…

Educated Pessimism. Then, you go over the top of the roller-coaster, and you hit Educated Pessimism. For some, this stage comes slowly and almost unnoticed at first. For others, it hits like a ton of bricks. You wake up one day and think, "Oh my goodness, I can't do this!"

However it comes about, there's a day when the new entrepreneur feels completely overwhelmed with the task he or she took on. The weight is not coming off as fast as you knew it would and the "diet" is just not something you can do one more day.

This is where real, clinical depression may set in. In the business world, it actually has a name – Entrepreneurial Depression. Here are some of the symptoms you (or loved ones nearest you) may notice:

- You feel sad or empty. Maybe even crying a lot.
- You have lost interest in things that use to grab your attention.
- You might gain or lose more than 5% of your weight.
- You notice you are either not sleeping at all or sleeping way too much.
- You are always just plain agitated about everything.
- You find you have no energy to do anything.
- You feel worthless or, even, guilty about how things are going in the business.
- You find it hard to think or concentrate.
- And, worst of all (when things are really extreme), you have suicidal thoughts

Pit of Despair. This is where most people make a critical decision. Eventually, you get to this crisis point. This is the point where you decide whether or not you are going to quit (you just don't have "it" in you to be an entrepreneur/to lose weight/to grab that dream you have had all your life, whatever "it" is).

This is where the vast majority of entrepreneurs quit (90% of them). This is where most diet and exercise programs fail. If someone does quit here, I call it crash and burn. The saddest decision is, if you quit. Your dream, your quest, is shattered. It breaks my heart when I see this happen because, as we will see shortly, it doesn't have to end this way.

Have you ever heard the statistic that 90% of new businesses fail? This is where the 90% (that's 9 out of every 10 people who try to be an entrepreneur) quit!

Educated Optimism. Or, you stick it out and become

successful. You figure it out, probably by getting proper mentors and coaches. You move into the promised land. Here's where it gets good. You figured out what you didn't know and apply it as fast as you can. Then, magic happens. Your company starts to take off. You are making a profit. The diet feels right. The weight is starting to come off. Your clothes are getting loose. That excitement you had the first day you felt that dream, it comes back. This is the way you thought it should be.

So, why is it no one knows about this roller coaster until it happens to them? And, what can we do to avoid it? I have no idea why no one hears about this until it happens to them. But, I assure you, the ***7 PERFECT Steps to Success*** can beat this roller coaster into the ground!

Protect the Dream

So, all of this begs the question: How do I avoid this pessimism and what do I do if it happens anyway? How do I protect the dream?

The good news is, if you implemented what you have learned in this book, you have done more than 99% of the people out there to insulate you from the downturn of the curve.

I wish I could say what you have learned in this book will make the success curve completely flat or always going up. But, that is just not how life works. I can almost guarantee you will go through the Educated Pessimism phase. The main difference between you and everyone else, though, is you have the tools to combat the effects and to minimize their impact on pursuing your dream.

How to Recognize the Attack

When you built your strategic and tactical plans, you and your coach put into it everything you could think of. You tried to cover every contingency. But, of course, you couldn't think of everything. Something will come up that was unexpected and seemingly large.

You will have some sort of emotional response to the situation. Depending on how you deal with stress, you might get angry or hyper or scared or sad. But, you will feel something. When you feel that (or, perhaps a spouse, friend, or business partner will notice and tell you) then look for what is going wrong in your business. Once you pin down the cause of the irritation, it's time to apply the fix.

How to Mitigate the Attack

The two biggest tools you have in your arsenal are your *Precious Burning Desire* and your *Effective Planning.*

Precious Burning Desire. Turning your dream into something big, like we talked about in the first chapter, will cause you not to even notice most obstacles. But, when an obstacle gets big enough to gain your attention, it's time to re-engage that dream.

The best tools for doing that come from *Chapter III: Repeat After Me.* You need to become your own cheer leader and pump yourself up. Look at your dream board. Maybe redo it completely. Come up with new positive affirmations for getting through this particular obstacle. Refocus on the prize and not the problem.

Remember your "why," and continue to tell yourself your "why."

Effective Planning. Usually, an obstacle that is big enough to trigger negative reaction comes about because we didn't know how to plan for it or didn't even know we should have planned for it. What you need to do is go back to your *Firsthand Knowledge* to see where the holes are so you can modify your plan and continue on. You may even need to find a new expert with the knowledge you need.

Before you take action, you should record the actions you want to take in both your strategic plan and your tactical plan. Years ago, when Cathy was getting her MBA, she took a course on process improvement. One of the things they emphasized in the course was repeatability and accountability. The best way to accomplish this is to record everything you want to do before you do it. And, change the fewest variables possible.

You have a good plan – especially if you had a coach or mentor help you put it together. So, you probably don't want to throw the whole thing out and start over. You probably don't even what to change large portions of it. Make small changes, check to see if they work, and do this as fast as you can.

The bottom line is, you have prepared for making your dream a reality. You know the **7 *PERFECT Steps to Success***. You are on your way to making it REAL! Don't let anything get in your way. You can do this!

Case Study I: Evangelist

I never thought it would happen in a Christian

ministry. The executive director of the first non-profit I had started (my baby) stole money from the company. And, it didn't stop there. He started a shadow company, using our name, and telling our customers he had taken over (with my blessing) and he would be the one they should all exclusively do business with for now on.

The damage to the company was extensive. Actually, it was catastrophic. It really was enough to make a person lose faith in humanity, quit life, and move to an island somewhere.

But, I couldn't do that – my dream was way too big to just give up. Instead, what I did was re-evaluate everything I had learned in building my first non-profit – both the things we did right and all the things we could have done better. I then relaunched my ministry as the ***Lura B Walker Foundation*** and rebranded the evangelism program to be called *Everyday Evangelism.*

Case Study 2: Real Estate Investing

Wow, our real estate investment companies were doing great. We were actively buying properties as fast as we could find them. We had investors lined up and banks who were happy to work with us. Everything was going gang busters.

An opportunity to buy a bundle of duplexes came up. It was out of state but that wasn't a problem, we actually own only one property in the state we live in. But, we needed to jump on it and we were in the middle of something else. I wanted the properties but I didn't want to go out and look at them myself – I'm sure you can see disaster coming.

Here was my thought process. The wholesaler who was offering me the properties had a good reputation. I had bought several properties from her before. I had a property manager out there who could look over the properties for rental opportunities. I also had a contractor in the area I had used on several occasions to rehab houses for me. He could look them over for any deferred maintenance.

I felt pretty good with these three team members looking over the properties for me. Big mistake. All of them are great people, they just all had different agendas than I did. We bought the properties on their word that the duplexes were "great." They were a disaster.

I won't go into all the problems (if you see me at a ***Life Changers 180*** conference, I'll tell you the whole story). But, almost right away, depression set in over these deals. It was so bad, I had fleeting thoughts of not doing any more deals – irrational, but honest. Fortunately, I had Tenacious Persistence and I was determined to stay in the business.

The fix to our tactical plan was, actually, quite easy. You may have already thought of it yourself. Never again would we but a property that we did not see with our own eyes.

Case Study 3: Getting in Shape

If you have ever tried to lose weight, you are probably very familiar with the success curve. Things go great, things go not so great, things go great again. Maybe it's because it is my actual body and, therefore, more intimate to me. But, when I fail at getting in shape it hits me harder than any of my other dreams.

When I was in my 20's and 30's it was so easy for me to be fit. In my 20's I was VERY active in martial arts – there were times I worked out 8-10 hours a day! I could eat anything and my six-pack remained. Then, in my 30's, I worked as a professional ball room dancer and instructor. Again, staying in shape was just natural.

Then, in my early 40's I messed up my shoulder. The doctor said the A/C joint of my right shoulder was worn down from too much bench pressing. I needed to have about an inch of my clavicle taken off. I stopped exercising for several months as I went through surgery and rehab. But, the spirit was gone. I had started to gain weight. And, since I wasn't exercising, other things took the time slots I had reserved for the gym. Life got in the way.

Fast forward to today. I found myself 100 pounds overweight! What!? When did THAT happen? I tried to get back in shape. Sometimes I would lose weight but I would always (and, I mean ALWAYS) gain it back. And, I would quit. Of course, this caused me to weigh more after the failed experiment than before.

This last time was different, though. When I would find myself falling back and failing, I would re-do my dream board and re-evaluate where the problems were. Then, I could work over my strategic and tactical plans to move me back toward success.

Exercises

As a final exercise in this book, write out your *Precious Burning Desire*, below, then GO FOR IT!!!

Final Thoughts

There's a story about a group of military recruiters who were invited to a high school assembly to talk to the students about serving their country.

The Army recruiter got up and talked for 15 minutes about being a force of one. He talked about the Green Beret and Airborne Rangers. Once he sat down, the Navy recruiter got up and, for 20 minutes, he talked about "Join the Navy and see the world." He talked about flying fighter jets off of aircraft carriers and about the Navy Seals. Next up, the Air Force recruiter. "Aim High" was his pitch. He talked about everything from fighter/bombers to having our finger on the trigger in a missile silo. After about 15 minutes, he sat down.

Finally, the Marine recruiter took center stage. He walked to the front of the platform, ramrod straight and at attention. He scanned the audience, looking each student in the eye as his head moved left to right, right to left.

After a few minutes, his head stopped and he opened his mouth to speak. "From at I can tell, only 5 of you have what it takes to be a Marine. I will be standing at my table in the hallway after this meeting to sign you up." That was all he said.

Just about every student in the room ran to his table to sign up, claiming they were one of the five.

If you have made it to this part of the book,

YOU HAVE WHAT IT TAKES TO BE SUCCESSFUL!

Whatever your *Precious Burning Desire*,
you CAN do it!

EPILOGUE

In this book I have talked about the ***7 PERFECT Steps to Success***. We have talked about the inside steps (desire and faith), the transitional steps (speaking, knowledge, and planning) and we have talked about the outside steps (decisiveness and persistence). If you follow these simple steps you WILL be successful in this life. But, no matter how successful you are, unless you follow the ***next*** 4 steps you will have done it all in vain.

There are really only two places we can spend eternity - heaven or hell. The Bible says, "*He that believeth on the Son hath everlasting life: and he that believeth not the Son shall not see life; but the wrath of God abideth on him.*" (John 3:36)

Eternal life, that's another term for heaven. Hell, that is the abiding wrath of God. And notice, the discriminator is what you do about Jesus. Let me explain.

STEP 1: UNDERSTAND ALL OF US ARE SINNERS.

The Bible tells us that we "*all have sinned and come short of God's glory.*" (Romans 3:23). Sin is basically doing something God tells us not to do. Sin in our life is like garbage in a garbage can. If you have an egg shell in the can or a gallon milk jug it's all still trash. It doesn't matter if it's small or large. Our sin is the same way – small or big, it's still sin and God can't let it into heaven. I've talked to people from all over the world and in all walks of life. Everyone has an understanding that they sin and are sinners. Can you think of some sins you have done in your life?

STEP 2: UNDERSTAND THERE IS A PUNISHMENT FOR OUR SINS.

We also know, instinctively, there are consequences to our sins. The Bible says, "*The wages of sin is death.*" (Romans 6:23a) Wages is what we earn for the work we do. If I did a great week's work and my boss refused to pay me, I would be upset. I worked for that money. I deserve that money. They are my wages. The Bible tells us the wages we have earned for our sins is a death penalty. And, when the Bible talks about death, it is more than just being placed in the ground at the end of life. The Bible talks about this death as the abiding wrath of God (John 3:36) in the lake of fire (Revelation 20:14).

STEP 3: UNDERSTAND JESUS PAID THE PRICE FOR OUR SINS.

But, does this mean all of us are destined to spend eternity in this lake of fire and never have a chance of going to heaven. Fortunately, no. The Bible says, "*But God commendeth his love toward us, in that, while we were yet sinners, Christ died for us.*" (Romans 5:8) It also says, "*For God so loved the world that He gave His only begotten Son that whosoever believes in Him should not perish but have everlasting life.*" (John 3:16) Basically, these verses are saying that Jesus, somehow, is willing to take our punishment for us so we can go to heaven.

Jesus died on a cross and, three days later, He rose from the dead. When he rose from the dead, it proved two things. First, it proved that He was and is God. No one who has been dead for three days can raise from the dead. Second, it proved that God the Father accepted His sacrifice for our sins.

Here's a good way to look at it. Pretend you have been arrested for robbing a bank. The trial happened, you were found guilty and you are standing before the judge for sentencing. As the judge pronounces your punishment and starts to hit the gavel, your best friend stands up in the back of the courtroom. He says, "Your honor, I am willing to take my friend's punishment." In order for your friend to take your punishment, three people must agree. The judge must agree to shift your punishment from you to your friend. Your friend must agree to take your punishment. And, finally, you must agree to let your friend take your punishment.

Salvation (getting to heaven through Jesus) is pretty much the same. God the Father has already agreed to let Jesus take your punishment. Jesus has already taken your punishment. His death on the cross was the payment for your sins - yes, it has already been paid. The only person left to agree to this deal is you.

STEP 4: ACCEPT WHAT JESUS DIED ON THE CROSS FOR YOU.

So, all you have to do is accept the price Jesus has already paid for your sins. The Bible says, "*For whosoever shall call upon the name of the Lord shall be saved.*" (Romans 10:13)

Have you ever flown in an airplane? When you get in the plane you turn to the right to find your seat. On the left, as you come in, is the cockpit – where the pilot sits. You've never met him, you don't know where he went to school for pilot training - you don't even know if he has a pilot's license. But, you are going to put your life in the hands of a man you've never met and trust him completely to get you somewhere you want to be. Trusting in Jesus is the same. You need to put your life in the hands of a man you've never met, Jesus, and trust what He did on the cross to get you someplace (heaven) that you want to be.

BOTTOM LINE

Do you believe you have sinned? Do you believe there is a punishment for sin? Do you believe Jesus died on a cross to take that punishment then, three days later, rose from the dead?

If you can answer yes to all of those questions, there is only one last question I have to ask you:

If Jesus is willing to accept you just the way you are, and He is, would you be willing to trust Him and accept Him as your only way to heaven?

If you want to put your trust in Jesus, you can say this simple prayer to invite Him to be your savior:

> God, I know that I am a sinner.
> I know that Jesus died on the cross for my sins.
> Please forgive me of my sins.
> Come into my life and my heart to save me.
> I ask the best I know how.
> In Jesus name, Amen.

Now, I want to share one more thing with you.

The Bible says "*That whosoever shall call upon the name of the Lord shall be saved.*" (Rom 10:13) Who do you think "whosoever" is? That's anybody in the world, that's me, that's you. Did you just call on the name of the Lord?

This passage says that whosoever (that's you) shall call on the name of the Lord (that's what you just did) shall be saved. So, according to God's Word, are you a saved person or a lost person? That's right, you are a saved person. Where do you think saved people go? That's right, to heaven. So, if you were to die tonight, you would spend eternity in heaven!

Do me a favor. This is the most important decision you will ever make. I would love to celebrate it with you. Can you drop me a letter or an email letting me know that you've trusted Jesus as your Savior? Here's my contact information: BobDudley@LifeChangers180.com

Now, go after that *Precious Burning Desire* with ALL your heart!

Life Changers 180, LLC is a premier success coaching and mentoring company. The core belief of LC180 is that every single person on the planet has a dream in their heart that CAN be realized.

We help people in all walks of life to see their dreams become a reality.

Some of our more popular offerings:

> ***Ignite Your Business***: Have you tried to build your own company only to find out it was a LOT harder than you expected? We can help!
>
> ***Ignite Your Fitness***: Have you tried EVERY diet and exercise program and just gotten more and more frustrated? Let us show you the "secret" to fitness success!
>
> ***Ignite Your Soul***: How can I have, how can you have, a close relationship with God? Is there a secret to peace and wisdom? We can guide you!

Our Life Changing Coaches and Mentors have DECADES of Experience to share with you! From bestselling authors, self-made millionaires, business professionals, fitness experts, and a spiritual guide/evangelist - we are uniquely positioned to help YOU be successful with your Dream.

Visit us at **www.LifeChangers180.org**

Or, on Facebook at **www.Facebook.com/LifeChangers180**

This is Madison Strempek's first book AND it is a #1 bestseller. AND, if that wasn't enough, Madison wrote this book when she was 10-years-old!

When Madison was trying to learn how to cope with her daddy going to prison, she could not find any books out there written for a child BY a child. She told her mom, "If there aren't any books for me, I'll just write one myself. Children need to know they are not alone."

Everyone Makes Mistakes: Living With My Daddy In Jail is the result of that effort. Here is what people are saying about this VERY special young lady:

"Your voice is important, and I trust you will keep working hard to pursue your dreams. I want you to hold on to the optimism and resolve that have brought you this far, and I am confident you will continue to do great things."

President of the United States of America, Barack Obama

"Your intro of Attorney General, Loretta Lynch was 100%, Madison. Thanks for speaking up for your dad and other kids of incarcerated parents."

Author of "Orange is the New Black," Piper Kerman

Everyone makes Mistakes:

Living With My Daddy In Jail ...

... is available online at

www.Amazon.com

www.BarnesAndNoble.com

This is Robin's perspective of the story told so preciously by Madison.

When Madison was trying to learn how to cope with her daddy going to prison, Robin was trying to learn how to lovingly guide her daughter through the most devastating event in Madison's life.

Everyone Makes Mistakes: A Parent's Perspective is a heart-to-heart discussion of Robin's struggles as she deals with helping Madison come to grips with these changes in her life.

If you have read Madison's book (**Everyone Makes Mistakes: Living with My Daddy in Jail**), you already know Robin got it right. But, how did she do it and what struggles did she go through? This book will give you all the answers. But, bring a box of tissues. She opens her heart.

You are both going to help so any parents and children who are going through the same thing. - Danielle

You are one strong woman and an excellent mother and role model. - Michelle

Everyone makes Mistakes:

A Parent's Perspective ...

... is available online at

www.Amazon.com

www.BarnesAndNoble.com

ABOUT THE AUTHORs

Bob Dudley is a retired Air Force Officer and co-founder of *Life Changers 180, LLC.* Bob spends most of his time on curriculum development. He also helps on stage with *Ignite Your Life* and *Ignite the World.*

Cathy Dudley is a mentor for *Life Changers 180, LLC.* Cathy has an MBA and a Masters in Biblical Studies. She also has over 25 years mentoring others. Her focus is on helping people with spiritual growth.

Bob and Cathy live in Hanover, PA with Little Buddy (their Pomeranian). When they are not helping people achieve their dreams, you can probably find them on the dance floor or a cruise ship.

Made in the USA
Columbia, SC
03 September 2018